WHAT PEOPLE ARE SAYING ABOUT MELVIN PILLAY

"Melvin, I love your enthusiasm. What a privilege it is for you to be here with us, where you also honored God so wonderfully well and so excitingly."

—**Zig Ziglar**

"Melvin Pillay is a gifted life coach who knows how to unlock the best out of any individual with love and care."

—**Ambassador Samuel Fidelis**

"Understanding success is one of the major challenges of today's world. Melvin Pillay shares how to gain true success not only at work but also at home. This teaching results from Melvin's practical living, which came from more than twenty-five years of research on this topic."

—**Tamrat Layne, Former Prime Minister of Ethiopia**

Melvin Pillay has a unique ability to awaken purpose and possibility in every person he encounters. He blends wisdom, faith, and real-world experience in a way that challenges you to rise higher and believe bigger. Every conversation with Melvin becomes a catalyst for growth, clarity, and renewed ambition. He doesn't just inspire—he activates the greatness already inside you.

—Daniel Ilea,
President of the Entrepreneurs Association,
Sibiu, Romania

Melvin Pillay carries a rare clarity and conviction that awakens purpose in every person he encounters. He doesn't just speak truth—he activates destinies.

—Christophe Dessaigne
Entrepreneur, Strategic Advisor & TEDx Speaker
Grenoble, France

We want to express our heartfelt gratitude to Melvin Pillay. His peaceful yet powerful presence is truly contagious, inspiring those around him to strive for greatness. Melvin's teachings and mindset on "unwork" have not only transformed both our lives but have also made a significant impact in the boardroom. Most importantly, his wisdom and character motivate us to become better people and more effective leaders. Thank you, Melvin, for your invaluable guidance and support on this journey of creating a life of significance.

—Jack and April Tu,
Toronto, Ontario

Melvin Pillay has a remarkable ability to motivate and activate everyone he encounters, inspiring teams to achieve their full potential.

—Thomas Kraus,
President of Embassy Connections,
Sibiu, Romania

Melvin Pillay is a living testimony to the transformative power of rest, demonstrating how proper recovery can significantly boost mental clarity, physical health, and overall well-being.

—Captain Peter Twang,
former Singapore Airlines A380 captain, Co-Founder of the Asia
Aeronautical Training Academy (AATA). Singapore

Melvin Pillay personifies wisdom and motivation. His own story from slum to success uniquely qualifies him to connect with challenges and inspire truly remarkable outcomes authentically.

—Andrew J Rodgers,
CEO & C-Suite Coach
London, United Kingdom

Do you ever find that reaching success is a never-ending pursuit? Then you need *Success Reimagined*. After our Whiteboard Destiny Session with Melvin, my wife and I had clarity of purpose. Melvin's perspective began to reshape our life philosophy radically. I encourage you to explore *Success Reimagined* and how it can shift your mindset from chasing success to reimagining what it means to be victorious!

—Stephen Sterne,
Speaker and Author of Grace Even After.
Howe, Texas

I could write a book about the impact Melvin Pillay has had on my life. After more than forty years as an entrepreneur—and countless hours and dollars spent trying to "fix" my weaknesses—Melvin did something remarkable in our very first White Board Session. He helped me see that God had already equipped me with everything I need to fulfill my purpose.

His coaching changes the way I work and lead. I've stopped spending time on tasks I wasn't created to do and now confidently reach out to other leaders to explore collaborations that multiply our impact. Together We Are Better!

—Barbara Hemphill
Founder, Productive Environment Institute
Raleigh, North Carolina

SUCCESS
REIMAGINED

How the Next Generation of Leaders
Will Redefine Life, Work Less, Produce More,
and Leave a Legacy That Lasts

MELVIN PILLAY

CONTENTS

To every leader, dreamer, builder, and believer who refused
to accept an outdated definition of success.
This book is for the ones who choose courage over
comfort, purpose over pressure, and destiny over doubt.
May you rise into your reimagined life.

FOREWORD

There's a conversation happening in boardrooms, living rooms, and coffee shops all over the world right now. It's a conversation about what really matters. About what success actually means. About whether the life we're building is the life we actually want to live.

And friend, it's about time we had this conversation.

For decades, we've been sold a vision of success that looks impressive on the outside but feels hollow on the inside. We've been taught that more is always better: more hours, more hustle, more sacrifice. We've measured our worth by our productivity and our significance by our exhaustion. We've climbed ladders only to discover they were leaning against the wrong walls.

I've spent my life helping people understand that you can have everything in life you want if you will just help enough other people get what they want. But here's what I've learned: if you don't know *who you are* while you're climbing, you'll reach the top and wonder why it feels so empty.

That's why this book matters.

Melvin Pillay has written something rare and remarkable. A book that challenges everything we thought we knew about success while honoring the dignity of hard work, the power of ambition, and the necessity of contribution. This isn't a book that tells you to work less and want less. This is a book that shows you how to work *right* and live *fully*.

Melvin's story grabbed me from the first page. Here's a man who escaped apartheid, broke free from generational poverty, built a life of impact and influence—and then had the courage to ask the hardest question of all: *What if I'm winning at the wrong game?*

That kind of honesty takes guts.

That kind of transformation takes wisdom.

And that kind of message? That's exactly what this generation—and every generation—needs to hear.

See, the world has changed. The old formulas no longer work. The next generation isn't rejecting success; they're rejecting *our version* of success. They're not lazy, they're looking for meaning. They're not entitled—they're exhausted by expectations that were never theirs to carry in the first place. They're struggling to navigate this new world. They're caught between what worked before and what's needed now. They're tired. They're confused. And deep down, many of them are wondering if there's a better way.

There is.

Melvin calls it alignment. I call it living with purpose. Whatever you call it, it's the difference between a life that looks successful and a life that *feels* successful. Between doing great things and becoming a great person. Between building an empire and building a legacy that actually matters.

In *Success Reimagined*, Melvin doesn't just tell you what's wrong with the old model; he gives you a blueprint for the new one. His frameworks aren't abstract theories; they're practical tools forged in the fire of real leadership, real failure, and real transformation. The UNWORK model, the Smart Work Matrix, the Power of 8, the Genius Zone—these aren't just concepts. They're the keys to unlocking a version of success that doesn't require you to sacrifice your health, your relationships, or your soul.

This book will challenge you. It will comfort you. It will make you rethink everything you thought you knew about what it means to win.

But most importantly, it will give you permission to stop performing and start living.

Permission to lead differently.

Permission to work smarter.

Permission to build a life that reflects who you really are, not just what you can produce.

I believe that success is not a destination; it's a direction. And the direction Melvin Pillay points us toward in this book is one worth following. It's a path that honors our ambition while protecting our humanity. A path that drives excellence without demanding exhaustion. A path that says you can have impact *and* peace, achievement *and* alignment, productivity *and* purpose.

That's not just a better way to succeed.

That's a better way to live.

So read this book carefully. Read it courageously. Read it with an open mind and a willing heart. Let it challenge your assumptions. Let it shift your perspective. Let it reimagine what's possible for your life, your leadership, and your legacy.

Because the world doesn't need more people sacrificing themselves at the altar of achievement.

The world needs more people like you—fully alive, fully aligned, and fully committed to a version of success that actually works.

This book will show you how.

Now let's get started.

Choose To Win!

—Tom Ziglar
CEO Zig Ziglar Corporation

PREFACE

For decades, I have watched leaders at every level—CEOs, professionals, entrepreneurs, parents, and government officials—struggle under an outdated definition of success. A definition built on exhaustion, fear, comparison, and pressure. A definition that promised fulfillment, yet delivered burnout. A definition so deeply ingrained in society that many never questioned whether a better way existed.

Until now.

We are living in a world undergoing unprecedented change. Technology has evolved. Expectations have evolved. The workforce has evolved. The next generation has evolved. Yet for far too long, our definition of success has remained frozen in time—anchored to old beliefs about hard work, sacrifice, and achievement at any cost.

Over the past 25 years, through coaching leaders, training organizations, and working with thousands across the globe, one truth has become clear:

The problem is not that people don't want to succeed.
The problem is that they've been taught the wrong version
of success.

This book exists to fix that.

Success Reimagined is not a theory. It is a blueprint—for life, for leadership, for work, for identity, and for purpose. It is the culmination of my coaching frameworks: The Smart Work Matrix, the principles of UNWORK, the Power of 8, and the lived experiences of countless people who were brave enough to question the old system.

I wrote this book for the leaders who are tired of grinding without meaning.

For the young adults who refuse to live the way their parents did.
For the professionals who feel trapped in roles that don't reflect who they are becoming.
For the CEOs who are trying to lead a workforce that thinks differently.
For the parents raising a generation that values purpose over pressure.
For the dreamers, builders, innovators, and changemakers who know there must be a better way.

And for you.

This book is an invitation—not to work less, but to live more.
Not to abandon success, but to redefine it.
Not to reject ambition, but to elevate it.
Not to run harder, but to run wiser.
Not to fit into the world, but to rise above it.

The next chapter of your life requires a new mindset, a new model, and a new understanding of what it means to win.

Success Reimagined is that model.

My hope is that as you turn these pages, you feel permission to breathe again.

That you discover clarity where you once felt confusion.

That you unlock strength where you once felt pressure.

And that you realize success was never about working harder—it was always about becoming more aligned, more purpose-driven, and more human.

You are standing at the doorway of a reimagined life.

Step forward.

Rise higher.

Lead boldly.

And redefine what success means for you—and for the world.

—Melvin Pillay

THE SHACK AND
THE WINGS OF PROMISE—
MY FIRST DREAM WAS TO ESCAPE

I grew up in a tin shack in South Africa—walls made of metal sheets, a dirt floor, and a roof that leaked every winter. Poverty wasn't just our condition; it was our reality... and for many, it was their destiny.

But one afternoon, a plane flew overhead.

I stopped what I was doing and watched. The roar of those engines shook something inside me. Even as a child, I felt it:

"One day, I am going to fly *in* you and never stop flying."

Nobody around me believed that. Not my teachers. Not the system. Not the world I was born into. But I believed it. I had to. Sometimes belief is the only possession the poor truly own.

That vow carried me through discrimination, poverty, immigration, heartbreak, rejection, and a thousand challenges that tried to break me.

Years later, I boarded plane after plane—not as a dreamer looking up, but as a man traveling the world, speaking life into leaders, CEOs, and young people.

Every time I take off, I remember the little boy standing outside his broken shack...believing he was meant to rise.

FROM APARTHEID TO ALIGNMENT: THE JOURNEY THAT REIMAGINED MY LIFE

was born into a world that tried to define me before I could even define myself.

Growing up in apartheid South Africa, the boundaries of my life were drawn by laws, systems, and structures meant to limit who I could become. Poverty was not just a condition—it was an atmosphere. Lack was familiar. Struggle was normal. The message that society sent us was silent but strong: *People like you don't rise.*

But something inside me refused to accept that.

As a young boy, I discovered early that work—hard, relentless, unforgiving work—was my ticket out. I believed that if I could outwork everyone around me, I could outrun my circumstances. So I did. I worked with an urgency fueled by fear. Fear of remaining stuck. Fear of becoming invisible. Fear of living the same life generation after generation.

Work became my identity.
Work became my armor.
Work became my escape.
Work became the proof that I mattered.

And for a long time, it seemed to be working.

I climbed faster than others.
I earned more than was expected.
I impressed people who had once overlooked me.
I carried the weight of responsibility on my back and never complained.

Because in my mind, I wasn't just working for myself.
I was working for my family, my community, my future children, and an entire generation behind me.
I believed that sacrificing myself—my peace, my health, my joy—was noble.

But here is the truth I didn't know then:

You can run your entire life and still never arrive.

My work ethic was legendary.
But so was my burnout.
So was my exhaustion.
So was my internal emptiness—the kind that no achievement could fix.

I spent years believing I was building a better life for others, meanwhile losing the life that actually belonged to me.

Success became a finish line I could never reach.
Every milestone only raised the bar higher.

Every accomplishment required another sacrifice.
Every achievement cost me another piece of myself.

I didn't realize it at the time, but I was becoming wealthy in results and poor in identity.

My turning point came not in a boardroom or on a stage, but in a moment of painful clarity:

**Hard work had elevated my life...
but it had also enslaved my identity.**

That was the moment I began to question everything:

Why do we glorify burnout?
Why do we praise exhaustion?
Why do we measure success by struggle?
Why do we admire the ones who sacrifice their lives for work, yet ignore the ones who sacrifice work for their lives?
Why is working less seen as laziness... when working wisely is what creates real impact?

And perhaps the most important question of all:

What if the definition of success we inherited was never correct to begin with?

That question sparked an awakening that transformed my life.

Slowly, I began letting go of the old world I had built—the world of pressure, perfection, and performance—and stepped into a new one built on clarity, identity, peace, alignment, purpose, and impact.

A world where:

- I wasn't defined by what I produced.
- I wasn't valued by how much I sacrificed.
- I wasn't measured by busyness.
- I wasn't rewarded for exhaustion.

A world where success didn't crush me—it completed me.

For the first time in my life, I wasn't just working—I was *living*.
I wasn't just achieving—I was *aligning*.
I wasn't just performing—I was *becoming*.

This book is not just a collection of principles.
It is the journey of a boy born into oppression who became a man trapped in overwork—
and ultimately discovered freedom through a new kind of success.

A success not built on sacrifice, but on strategy.
Not on hustle, but on harmony.
Not on pressure, but on purpose.
Not on burnout, but on becoming whole.

The old definition of success was built for survival.
The new definition is built for significance.

And that is why I wrote this book.

Because millions of people across the world—CEOs, professionals, young leaders, parents, entrepreneurs—are still living with the same outdated definition that once ruled my life. A definition that is no longer relevant and no longer necessary.

I want to show you what I had to learn the hard way:

Success must be reimagined—
not because the world has changed,
but because *you* have.

The journey you are about to take is not just information—it is transformation.

From survival to significance.
From workaholic to aligned.
From exhausted to empowered.
From striving to rising.

Welcome to the life you were always meant to live.

Welcome to *Success Reimagined*.

THE LAST TWO DOLLARS

The Night My Destiny Cost Everything

I was alone in New Zealand with nothing but uncertainty and hunger pressing against me. I had almost no money left—just two dollars—and I stood in a public library wondering how I was going to survive another day.

I walked past the food stalls outside. My stomach was growling. But something drew me inside the library. Maybe desperation. Maybe hope. Maybe God.

That's when I saw it. A dusty old cassette tape tucked between outdated encyclopedias.
The label read:

"Zig Ziglar—See You at the Top."

I had no idea who Zig Ziglar was. But something in me whispered:

"Take it. This is for you."

Logic screamed that I should buy food. But destiny speaks in a different language.

I took my last two dollars—literally the final coins I had to my name—and paid the borrowing fee. I left the library hungry, but for the first time in months, I felt a spark.

I pressed play.

Zig's voice filled the room—and pierced my soul.

I cried.
I laughed.
I came alive again.

He spoke of identity, purpose, calling—things I had forgotten under the crushing weight of survival.

That $2 cassette didn't just inspire me—it ignited the life I live today. Years later, I would stand on global stages as a Zig Ziglar Platinum Speaker... the very legacy that began with two dollars and a broken cassette.

SUCCESS IS BROKEN

CHAPTER ONE

THE DEATH OF THE HARD WORK MYTH

For centuries, society has preached one unquestioned belief: "Hard work is the key to success."

But look closely at the world today—the people working the hardest are not the wealthiest, the happiest, or the most fulfilled. Many are exhausted, stressed, overwhelmed, and barely surviving.

Meanwhile, a new generation has emerged—one that refuses to sacrifice their health, joy, or sanity in the name of "hard work."

And this has frustrated parents, employers, managers, and CEOs everywhere.

They complain:

"Young people don't want to work anymore."

But the truth is far more profound:

They DO want to work.
They just refuse to work the old way.

They don't want work to be defined by exhaustion.
They don't want success defined by sacrifice.
They don't want productivity defined by pain.

To them, hard work is not heroic—it's outdated.

This new generation sees life differently:
they believe work should be meaningful, energizing, and aligned with purpose. Not a burden. Not a grind. Not a sentence.

Hard Work Built the Industrial Age.
Smart Work Will Build the Future.

The old formula was simple:

Work harder.
Work longer.
Be loyal.
Don't complain.
Keep your head down.
Grind until you die.

It produced factories, machines, and economic empires—but it also produced burnout, broken families, and workforce fatigue that spans generations.

Hard work made nations rich.
But it made people tired.

So How Did We Get Here?

We were raised on a very specific script:

"Work hard in school to get good grades."
"Work hard in college to get a good job."
"Work hard at your job so you can survive."
"Work hard in marriage—it's tough."
"Work hard raising your kids—it's difficult."
"Work hard at everything—life is hard."

Without realizing it, we inherited a philosophy of struggle.

Hard work became not just a habit—but an identity.

It shaped:
Our choices
Our careers
Our confidence
Our expectations
Our limits
Our beliefs about what is possible

But here's the truth many leaders overlook:

Hard work alone has never guaranteed success.
Otherwise, the hardest workers would be the wealthiest.

And history proves the opposite.

The New Generation Is Not Weak—
They Are Awakening

What older generations call laziness
is often simply clarity.

This generation doesn't want:

- meaningless labor
- unhealthy pressure
- outdated systems
- toxic expectations
- work that destroys their joy or identity

They want something better.

They want:

- creativity
- autonomy
- fulfillment
- purpose
- smart systems
- meaningful results

They want *Success Reimagined*.

And that desire is not a weakness—it is evolution.

The Real Question Is Not:
"Why don't they want to work?"

The real question is:
"Why are we still defining work the same way as the Industrial Revolution of 1760?"

The world has changed.
Economies have changed.
Technology has changed.

Expectations have changed.

People have changed.

But our philosophy of work has remained trapped in the past.

This book exists for one reason:

> *To redefine work, success, and productivity for the modern world—and to introduce a new blueprint for a life worth living.*

Because success isn't disappearing.

It is simply being reimagined.

CHAPTER TWO

WHY WORKING HARDER IS NO LONGER A COMPETITIVE ADVANTAGE

For decades, "work harder" was the universal prescription for success.

If you weren't winning, the solution was simple:
Put in more hours, more effort, more sacrifice.

But we now live in a world where harder is not faster...
where longer is not better...
And where effort alone does not guarantee excellence.

Today, the competitive advantage has shifted.

The future does not belong to the hardest worker.
It belongs to the smartest thinker.

And this truth is transforming industries, classrooms, boardrooms, and even family dynamics—especially in the way the younger generation views work.

Henry Ford's employee who "Sits and Thinks."

Henry Ford was famous for paying the highest salaries in the industry.

One day, a curious journalist asked him:

"Mr. Ford, who's the highest-paid person in your company?"

Ford smiled and took him on a tour of the enormous factory—workers everywhere, machines roaring, bells ringing, elevators going up and down.

A perfectly organized chaos.

Then, in the middle of the noise, there was a small, closed office.

Inside, a man sat comfortably in a chair, feet on the table, hat over his eyes—apparently doing nothing.

Ford knocked on the door.

The man lifted his hat slightly and said, "Hey, Henry, everything good?"

Ford nodded with a grin, closed the door, and kept walking.

The journalist was shocked.

"Who is that man?"

Ford chuckled.

"He's the highest-paid employee in the company."

The journalist frowned.

"But... what does he actually do?"

Ford replied:

"He does nothing. He comes in, sits down, and thinks."

Then he added:

"I hired him to think. Every new system, every car model idea—they all come from his mind.

He relaxes, reflects, and sends me his ideas.

I turn them into reality—and make millions.

Ideas are worth more than anything.

But to have them, you need time, silence, and mental space.

If you're busy all the time, you'll never create something new.

That's why I pay him to think."

The journalist was speechless—then applauded.

THE WORLD CHANGED— HARD WORK DIDN'T

To understand why hard work is losing its value, look at what has changed:

1. Technology multiplied productivity.

A single person today can do what once required 50 employees. Automation, AI, digital tools, and online systems can outperform human labor 24/7.

Hard work cannot compete with exponential technology.

2. Knowledge replaced muscle.

In the industrial age, strength won.
In the information age, strategy wins.

Those who think clearly outperform those who grind endlessly.

3. Creativity became the new currency.

Innovation now builds empires.
Ideas now change economies.
Your value is no longer in how much effort you can produce but in how much creativity you can generate.

4. Burnout became a global epidemic.

We simply cannot sustain the "work harder, sleep less" culture. Health, mental clarity, and emotional resilience have become leadership essentials.

5. People now value meaning, not misery.

This generation is not willing to sacrifice their joy for a paycheck.
They want alignment, purpose, fulfillment—not just survival.

Hard work without meaning is no longer appealing...
and no longer profitable.

THE GAME CHANGED—
BUT OUR BELIEFS DIDN'T

Even though the world evolved, the philosophy of work
stayed the same.

Older generations were conditioned to believe:

- Struggle is noble.
- Exhaustion is honorable.
- Sacrifice is admirable.
- Pain means you are progressing.
- The person who suffers the most deserves the most success.

But suffering is not a strategy.

Pain is not a business plan.
Exhaustion is not a competitive advantage.
Burnout is not a badge of honor—it is a warning sign.

We inherited a belief that effort equals success,
but the global marketplace now rewards something completely
different:

Efficiency, innovation, adaptability, and emotional intelligence.

This is why the younger generation refuses to play the old game.

THE YOUNGER GENERATION IS NOT LAZY— THEY ARE ADVANCED

While many leaders complain: "Kids today don't want to work," the truth is:

They don't want to work the old way.

This is not laziness—it is evolution.

They are asking the right questions:

- Why should I work 60 hours when I can accomplish the same in 20?
- Why should I grind when I can automate?
- Why should I burn out when I can balance?
- Why should I sacrifice my health for someone else's dream?
- Why should I repeat broken systems that don't work?

They are not avoiding work.
They are rejecting waste.

They don't want to work endlessly—
they want to work intelligently.

They don't want to chase arbitrary success—
they want a life of victory, impact, and freedom.

They are not the problem.
They are the pioneers of a new philosophy of work.

And the leaders who understand this will attract, motivate, and retain the best talent of the next generation.

THE DANGERS OF THE HARD-WORK OBSESSION

There are three major dangers leaders must understand:

1. **More work does not mean more results.**
   After a certain point, effort declines, and mistakes increase.

2. **Hard work creates dependence, not development.**
   People become good at labor, not leadership.
   Good at tasks, not thinking.
   Good at execution, not innovation.

3. **Hard work eventually kills creativity.**
   Fatigue shuts down inspiration.
   Stress shuts down imagination.
   Fear shuts down ambition.

A burned-out employee cannot innovate.
A stressed CEO cannot think.
A tired parent cannot lead.

THE NEW COMPETITIVE ADVANTAGE: THINKING

The future belongs to individuals who can:

- Think clearly
- create boldly

- adapt quickly
- innovate consistently
- lead compassionately
- work strategically
- operate from vision, not exhaustion

This is why *Success Reimagined* is not just a book. It is a philosophy shift.

A transformation.
A new way of living.
A new way of leading.
A new way of raising children.
A new way of building strong teams, healthy cultures, and sustainable success.

Because the leaders who will thrive in the new era are not those who work the hardest...

but those who redefine work altogether.

WORK IS NOT DEAD—BUT IT MUST EVOLVE

Work still matters—
but not in the way we were taught.

Hard work without strategy is wasted energy.
Hard work without clarity is misdirected effort.
Hard work without vision is empty.

But...

Work with purpose becomes commitment.
Work with intelligence becomes mastery.
Work with creativity becomes innovation.
Work with balance becomes sustainability.

The younger generation already understands this.
Now leaders must understand it too.

CHAPTER THREE

THE YOUNGER GENERATION ISN'T LAZY — THEY'RE LOGICAL

There was a time in my life when I believed the only way to prove my worth was through relentless hard work. I outworked everyone. I slept less. I hustled when everyone else rested. And the world rewarded me for it.

I climbed the corporate ladder faster than most.
I got the recognition, the influence, the salary—everything I thought I wanted.

But no one knew the truth.

Inside, I was empty.
Every morning, I woke up exhausted.
Every night, I went to bed anxious.
I was becoming successful on paper and lost in reality.

One morning, after yet another sleepless night, I looked into the mirror and saw a version of myself I didn't recognize—a man performing success instead of living it.

The question that hit me changed my life:

"What's the point of winning the world if I lose myself?"

That moment became my turning point.

I walked away—not because I was broken, but because I finally understood that success built on sacrifice without purpose is not success at all.

I chose alignment.
I chose identity.
I chose to redefine success on my own terms.

And that choice led me to build businesses, speak globally, and live with purpose—not pressure.

Every generation looks at the one behind them and sees something they don't understand.
For decades, parents, CEOs, business owners, and leaders have repeated the same complaint:

"Young people today don't want to work."

But that conclusion is not only inaccurate—it is dangerously misleading.

The younger generation is not lazy.
They are not entitled.
They are not unwilling.

They are logical.

They grew up in a different world with different rules, different pressures, and different opportunities. Their philosophy is not based on tradition—it is built on observation.

And the observation is simple:

The old system doesn't work.

THEY SEE WHAT OLDER GENERATIONS REFUSE TO ADMIT

To older generations, work is a badge of honor.
To younger generations, work is a tool—not an identity.

They watched the people they love:

- Work hard their entire lives
- Sacrifice their dreams
- Miss their children growing up
- Lose their health
- Lose their marriages
- Die young
- Retire tired
- Live unfulfilled

And for what?

A pension?
A title?
A gold watch?
A few weeks of vacation?
A lifetime of exhaustion?

The younger generation saw the cost of the "hard work" philosophy — and they made a logical decision:

"I will not repeat that."

THEY VALUE WHAT ACTUALLY CREATES SUCCESS

Young people today are not motivated by tradition—
they are motivated by results.

They care about:

- Meaning
- Balance
- Mental health
- Autonomy
- Creativity
- Human connection
- Purpose
- Freedom

They know that these ingredients create better performance, better lives, and better outcomes.

While older generations were rewarded for endurance, obedience, and loyalty...
the new generation is rewarded for innovation, adaptability, and creativity.

They are simply aligning their effort with what the world now rewards.

This isn't laziness—
it is intelligent alignment.

THEY ARE NOT AVOIDING WORK—
THEY ARE AVOIDING WASTE

This generation does not fear work.
They fear:

- meaningless work
- unproductive routines
- outdated processes
- toxic environments
- pointless meetings
- micromanagement
- rigid schedules
- lack of purpose
- low-impact effort

Why?

Because they believe what many leaders secretly know but refuse to say:

Hard work is not the same as useful work.

If a task can be automated, digitized, simplified, or eliminated, they will choose that path—not to avoid effort, but to produce results.

To them, efficiency is not cheating.
It is wisdom.

They don't want to look busy—
they want to be effective.

THEY WANT A NEW DEFINITION OF SUCCESS

Older generations were taught:

"Success = stability, career, salary, and sacrifice."

Younger generations define it differently:

"Success = freedom, impact, health, happiness, and purpose."

Neither definition is wrong—they are simply different.

But the younger generation's definition is more aligned with how the world now functions:

- Remote work
- Digital careers
- Multiple income streams
- Online entrepreneurship
- Tech-enabled lifestyles
- Global opportunities
- Flexible schedules
- Creative paths to wealth

The younger generation isn't rebelling—
they are evolving.

THEY GREW UP WATCHING THE WORLD CHANGE

Think about it:

Older generations were raised to operate machines.
Younger generations were raised to operate ideas.

Older generations were trained to follow systems.
Younger generations were trained to question systems.

Older generations valued structure.
Younger generations value strategy.

Older generations sought stability.
Younger generations seek scalability.

Older generations were shaped by factories.
Younger generations were shaped by technology.

These two mindsets are not oppositions.
They are two stages of progress.

And that is why leaders who understand this shift will always outperform leaders who resist it.

THEY WANT WHAT EVERY LEADER CLAIMS TO WANT

When leaders say, "young people don't want to work," what they really mean is:

They don't want to work under outdated expectations.

But what do young people actually want?

They want to:

- contribute
- create
- innovate
- learn
- grow
- excel
- make an impact
- be valued
- be trusted
- be challenged

Does that sound lazy?

Or does that sound like the future?

The truth is, they want exactly what every great company wants:

- high performance
- high engagement
- high creativity
- high impact

They just don't want to achieve it through burnout and misery.

And that perspective is not weakness—
it is wisdom.

LEADERS MUST EVOLVE—OR THEY WILL LOSE TALENT

Today's workforce has options.
If they feel trapped, undervalued, ignored, or micromanaged...
they will simply leave.

Not because they don't want to work—
but because they refuse to waste their potential.

And the most talented young people will not settle:

- They will build their own businesses.
- They will launch their own brands.
- They will find global opportunities.
- They will create digital careers.
- They will work for leaders who inspire, not demand.

In a world filled with choices,
poor leadership is no longer a prison—
it is simply a detour.

THEY ARE NOT THE PROBLEM—THEY ARE THE SOLUTION

The younger generation is signaling something older generations must recognize:

"The future of work must change."

And they are right.

The world has evolved.
Technology has evolved.
Economies have evolved.
Human needs have evolved.

Now work must evolve.

The younger generation is not rejecting responsibility.
They are rejecting outdated definitions of success.

They are not fighting against work.
They are fighting for a better kind of work.

And that is not rebellion—
it is leadership.

WORK, REDEFINED

CHAPTER FOUR

THE TRUE DEFINITION OF WORK: CREATE, SOLVE, CONTRIBUTE

For generations, society defined work as effort, labor, or physical activity.

Work meant motion.

Work meant sweat.

Work meant exhaustion.

But that definition is not only outdated—
it is dangerously limiting.

To build a thriving business, lead a successful organization, raise a strong family, or create an innovative future, we need a far more accurate and empowering definition of work.

Let's rewrite the foundation.

WORK IS NOT EFFORT. WORK IS IMPACT.

Work is not what you do.
Work is what your actions produce.

This means:

- You can be busy and achieve nothing.
- You can work long hours with little impact.
- You can put in effort without creating value.
- You can sweat all day and still stay stuck.

Effort is not the goal—
results are.

True work has three components:

1. CREATE
2. SOLVE
3. CONTRIBUTE

These are the pillars of modern productivity and the foundation of all meaningful success.

Let's break them down.

1. WORK = CREATE

The first form of work is creation.

To create is to bring something into existence that wasn't there before.

This could be:

- a new idea
- a new solution

- a new system
- a new strategy
- a new product
- a new opportunity
- a new business
- a new approach

Creation is the highest form of human work because creation multiplies value.

A single idea can change an entire industry.
A single invention can transform a generation.
A single insight can shift a nation.

Creation is what separates leaders from followers.
It separates thinkers from workers.
It separates innovators from imitators.

When you create, you are not working harder—
you are working higher.

And this is exactly what the younger generation values.
They don't want to be cogs in a system.
They want to design new systems.

That's not laziness.
That's leadership.

2. WORK = SOLVE

Every business, government, organization, or family exists to solve problems.

Problems are not obstacles—
they are opportunities for value creation.

When you solve a problem, you:

- increase your relevance
- increase your influence
- increase your income
- increase your impact
- increase your leadership

Problem solvers rise quickly because they make themselves indispensable.

This is why some people get hired easily, promoted quickly, and paid significantly more:

They solve meaningful problems.

Solving problems is the second-highest form of work.

Not because it requires effort—
but because it requires thinking.

Anyone can follow a checklist.
But not everyone can see solutions where others see chaos.

The world rewards thinkers—
not grinders.

3. WORK = CONTRIBUTE

The third form of real work is contribution.

Contribution means you bring value to a person, a team, an organization, or society.

Contribution takes many forms:

- supporting others
- communicating effectively
- improving culture
- sharing knowledge
- strengthening systems
- elevating performance
- inspiring change

Contribution is not measured in hours—
it is measured in impact.

A single contribution can outweigh months of effort.

For example:

A 30-minute conversation can save a team 3 months of confusion.

A single strategy can save a company millions.

One powerful speech can ignite an entire workforce.

One decision can change the trajectory of a business.

Contribution turns ordinary individuals into leaders.

Hard work may build you a career.
But contribution builds you a legacy.

WHY THIS NEW DEFINITION MATTERS

When leaders and parents understand that work is create, solve, and contribute, everything changes.

You stop asking:
"Why aren't you working harder?"

And start asking:
"What value are you creating?"
"What problem are you solving?"
"How are you contributing?"

This perspective empowers people instead of exhausting them.

It produces results instead of resistance.

And it helps you see the younger generation for who they really are:

Not unwilling...
but strategic.
Not avoiding work...
but redefining it.
Not entitled...
but enlightened.

HOW LEADERS CAN APPLY THIS RIGHT NOW

If you are a CEO, a manager, a business owner, or a parent, here is how to implement the new definition of work:

1. **Measure results, not hours.**
   Output is more important than effort.

2. **Encourage creation.**
   Ask for ideas, not just tasks.

3. **Reward problem-solving.**
   Celebrate innovation, not endurance.

4. **Build a culture of contribution.**
   Empower people to make a difference.

5. **Replace micromanagement with trust.**
   Autonomy creates excellence.

6. **Focus on strengths, not weaknesses.**
   People are most valuable where they are most gifted.

7. **Give purpose, not pressure.**
   People perform higher when they believe in what they're doing.

This is how modern leaders win.

THE YOUNGER GENERATION ALREADY THINKS THIS WAY

They don't want:

- meaningless jobs
- repetitive tasks
- unnecessary meetings
- fixed schedules
- outdated rules
- They want:
- to create
- to solve
- to contribute

They want to make an impact—not just an income.

They are not rejecting work;
they are rejecting a shallow definition of work.

They are choosing depth over repetition.
Clarity over tradition.
Meaning over motion.
Innovation over imitation.

This is not laziness—
this is evolution.

YOU CAN'T LEAD THE FUTURE
WITH THE PHILOSOPHIES OF THE PAST

The world is changing fast.
Organizations must change with it.

Parents must adapt.
Leaders must evolve.
Schools must innovate.
Businesses must modernize.

We cannot prepare the next generation for the future by clinging to the past.

The old definition of work created employees.
The new definition of work creates leaders.

And leaders are exactly who the world needs now.

CHAPTER FIVE

THE SHIFT FROM SUCCESS TO VICTORY

For decades, people have been chasing "success" without ever stopping to question what the word truly means.
It became the universal goal—the standard, the dream, the finish line.

But here's the truth most leaders eventually discover:

Success is vague.
Success is shallow.
Success is unstable.
Success is incomplete.

Success is a moving target shaped by culture, society, and external approval.
It depends on comparison, competition, and what others say is valuable.

And because of that, millions of people "succeed" yet still feel unfulfilled.

Success sounds noble.
But victory feels different.

SUCCESS IS WHAT THE WORLD APPLAUDS.
VICTORY IS WHAT YOUR SOUL CELEBRATES.

Success is external.
Victory is internal.

Success is a moment.
Victory is a lifestyle.

Success depends on conditions.
Victory depends on character.

Success needs validation.
Victory needs intention.

Success can be taken from you.
Victory cannot be touched.

You can lose success through:

- layoffs
- market shifts
- economic changes
- industry disruption
- personal setbacks
- life circumstances

But victory?
Victory lives inside you.

It is not something you earn—
it is something you become.

THE PROBLEM WITH CHASING SUCCESS

Success is fragile because its foundation is unstable.

Most people define success by:

- money
- titles
- awards
- recognition
- external approval
- followers
- status

But these things don't last.

How many executives, celebrities, professionals, and business owners appear successful on the outside but are:

- exhausted
- empty
- stressed
- lonely
- depressed
- overwhelmed
- uncertain
- quietly unhappy

Success without meaning is a quiet tragedy.
Success without joy is a hidden burden.
Success without purpose is failure dressed in a fancy suit.

This is why the world is filled with people who "made it" but still feel like something is missing.

VICTORY IS DIFFERENT

Victory is not measured by the world—
it is measured by the individual.

Victory happens when:

- You live aligned with your purpose
- You rise above excuses
- You embrace smart work
- You refuse to settle for less
- You build consistency
- You conquer your fears
- You stay true to who you are
- You pursue growth instead of comfort
- You create impact, not just income
- Victory is internal mastery, not external applause.

Success happens to you.
Victory happens because of you.

WHY THE YOUNGER GENERATION PURSUES VICTORY, NOT SUCCESS

Older generations were trained to chase success.
Younger generations are choosing victory.

This is why they are redefining work, redefining leadership, and redefining fulfillment.

They prioritize:

- mental wellness
- freedom
- flexibility
- meaningful work
- creativity
- self-expression
- purpose
- balance
- impact

They are no longer asking:

"How can I look successful?"

They are asking:

"How can I become victorious in every area of life?"

This shift terrifies traditional leaders because it challenges the old model:

- Work until you collapse.
- Retire when you're too tired to enjoy life.

- Stay loyal even when it hurts you.
- Chase goals society assigned you.
- Sacrifice your identity for achievement.
- This generation rejects that.

They want a life worth living—not a life spent proving something.

And that is not rebellion.
It is wisdom.

VICTORY IS SUSTAINABLE. SUCCESS IS NOT.

Success often demands:

- burnout
- sacrifice
- imbalance
- unrealistic pressure
- constant comparison
- endless competition
- Victory, however, requires:
- clarity
- resilience
- smart work
- emotional intelligence
- strategic thinking
- inner strength
- alignment
- purpose-driven action

Success drains you.
Victory develops you.

Success is measured by trophies.
Victory is measured by transformation.

Success is a momentary achievement.
Victory is a lifelong evolution.

THE THREE LEVELS OF VICTORY

Victory happens in three dimensions:

1. **Personal Victory**

   - Achieving mastery over:
   - Your thoughts
   - Your emotions
   - Your habits
   - Your choices
   - Your focus
   - Your self-belief

Without personal victory, professional success is hollow.

2. **Professional Victory**

Building a career or business that:

   - aligns with your strengths
   - expresses your creativity
   - contributes real value

- creates impact
- generates sustainable income
- reflects your authentic identity

This is where smart work replaces hard work.
Where efficiency replaces exhaustion.
Where innovation replaces imitation.

3. Legacy Victory

This is the highest form of victory.

It is the victory that outlives you.

Legacy victory is about:

- people you empower
- lives you influence
- culture you improve
- ideas you contribute
- systems you build
- opportunities you create
- the next generation you prepare

Legacy victory is the greatest outcome of smart leadership.

It is the ultimate proof that you lived with intention, purpose, and impact.

LEADERS WHO CHASE SUCCESS BUILD COMPANIES.

LEADERS WHO CHASE VICTORY BUILD CIVILIZATIONS.

Success ends when the applause stops.
Victory continues through the people you've influenced long after you're gone.

Success makes you known.
Victory makes you remembered.

Success builds a career.
Victory builds a legacy.

This book is not teaching you how to be successful.

It is teaching you how to be victorious.

Because the world doesn't need more people who "made it."

The world needs more people who became it.

CHAPTER SIX

SMART WORK VS HARD WORK: THE NEW RULES

For generations, hard work was the gold standard.
The ultimate virtue.
The non-negotiable requirement for success.

Parents preached it.
Bosses demanded it.
Schools celebrated it.
Society idolized it.

But the world has changed—dramatically.
And with it, the rules of success have radically shifted.

Today, hard work alone is no longer enough, and in many cases, it is the slowest, least effective, and most exhausting path to progress.

The new competitive advantage—the one used by top CEOs, innovators, high performers, and the younger generation—is something far more powerful:

Smart Work.

Let's break down exactly what that means and why it's transforming the future of leadership, business culture, and human potential.

THE OLD RULES OF HARD WORK

Most people were raised under the following beliefs:

The more hours you work, the more successful you'll be.

If you want better results, increase your effort.

Sacrifice is a sign of commitment.

Productivity is measured in time, not results.

Rest is a reward you earn, not a necessity you need.

The "grind" is the only path to greatness.

These rules created structure, discipline, resilience, and progress... but they also created burnout, exhaustion, and a generation of people who achieved success at the cost of their health, joy, and identity.

Hard work made nations strong—
but it made individuals tired.

THE NEW RULES OF SMART WORK

Smart work is not necessarily about working less.
It is about working right.

It is intentional.
Purposeful.
Efficient.
Strategic.
Focused.
Measured.
Creative.

Smart work produces more results with less stress.
More progress with less pressure.
More impact with less burnout.

Let's compare the difference.

HARD WORK VS SMART WORK

1. Hard Work = Effort
Smart Work = Strategy

Hard work says, "Do more."
Smart work says, "Think more."

Effort without strategy is wasted energy.
Strategy without effort becomes brilliance in motion.

2. Hard Work = Time
Smart Work = Results

Hard workers pride themselves on long hours.
Smart workers pride themselves on meaningful outcomes.

In today's world, results outweigh time.

A person who accomplishes in 2 hours what others do in 10 is not lazy—they are highly valuable.

3. Hard Work = Repetition
Smart Work = Innovation

Hard work relies on doing the same thing over and over.
Smart work asks, "How can this be done better?"

Innovators are not always harder workers—
they are better thinkers.

4. Hard Work = Force
Smart Work = Flow

Hard work pushes.
Smart work aligns.

When work aligns with your strengths, passions, and natural abilities, productivity becomes effortless and sustainable.

The younger generation understands this deeply.

5. Hard Work = Sacrifice
Smart Work = Sustainability

Hard work often sacrifices:

- sleep
- relationships

- health
- creativity
- mental clarity

Smart work protects these things because they fuel long-term performance.

A burned-out leader makes bad decisions.
A stressed parent becomes reactive.
An exhausted employee becomes ineffective.

Smart work is not just a method—
it is a lifestyle.

6. Hard Work = "Do it yourself."
Smart Work = "Leverage systems."

Hard work believes:

"I must be the one to do everything."

Smart work believes:

"If I can automate it, systemize it, delegate it, relegate it, or eliminate it—I should."

Smart workers use:

- technology
- automation
- project management tools
- checklists
- templates
- outsourcing

- collaboration
- mentorship
- AI
- digital leverage

Not to avoid work...
But to accelerate excellence.

7. *Hard Work = Survive.*
Smart Work = Scale.

Hard workers maintain.
Smart workers multiply.

Smart work creates:

- more freedom
- more income
- more innovation
- more opportunities
- more impact
- more growth
- more legacy

Hard work helps you survive.
Smart work helps you thrive.
Smart work done consistently helps you win.

WHY LEADERS MUST MAKE THE SHIFT NOW

The workforce has changed.
The economy has changed.
Expectations have changed.
Talent has changed.
Technology has changed.
Human psychology has changed.

But many leaders are still operating with a hard-work mindset in a smart-work world.

This creates friction:

- They push harder instead of thinking smarter.
- They demand output instead of cultivating innovation.
- They measure time instead of measuring impact.
- They reward exhaustion instead of excellence.
- They confuse busyness with productivity.

And when the younger generation resists these outdated practices, leaders assume it is rebellion.

It is not rebellion—
it is revelation.

This generation isn't rejecting work.
They are rejecting inefficient, outdated, uninspired work models.

THE YOUNGER GENERATION NATURALLY THINKS IN SMART WORK TERMS

Why?

Because they grew up in a world where:

- Technology multiplies effort
- Information is instantly accessible
- Tools simplify complex tasks
- Global Talent is a click away
- Creativity is rewarded
- Innovation is normal
- Automation is everywhere

They aren't trying to avoid work—
they're trying to optimize it.

They aren't afraid of hard work—
they just refuse to confuse pain with progress.

They want to work with:

- intention
- energy
- alignment
- impact
- creativity
- purpose

And that's exactly what leaders should want to.

THE FUTURE BELONGS TO SMART WORKERS

Look at the most successful companies, innovators, and leaders in the world:

- They don't grind endlessly.
- They don't stay busy for the sake of being busy.
- They don't reward suffering.
- They don't waste time.
- They don't micromanage.
- They don't operate in chaos.

Instead, they:

- leverage talent
- protect mental clarity
- use efficient systems
- focus on creative problem-solving
- drive with purpose
- maximize strengths
- eliminate unproductive tasks

This is smart work.
This is modern productivity.
This is the future.

SMART WORK MAKES WORK POWERFUL

Smart work does not eliminate work—
it elevates it.

When your work is aligned, intelligent, focused, and meaningful, work becomes fuel, not friction.

Smart work creates the environment where work actually pays off.

The combination of both produces unstoppable people.

THE NEW RULES OF WORK
(THE SMART WORK CODE)

Think first, act second.
Leverage technology.
Protect your energy.
Eliminate unnecessary tasks.
Use systems to create consistency.
Work in your strengths, not your struggles.
Create before you consume.
Focus on outcomes, not hours.
Learn constantly.

Measure progress weekly, not yearly.

This is how the world's top performers operate—
and how the next generation will lead.

THE HUMAN FACTOR

CHAPTER SEVEN

MENTAL HEALTH AND MODERN PRODUCTIVITY

For generations, productivity was measured by how much a person could endure.

How long they could work.

How much pressure they could carry.

How much stress they could absorb.

How much exhaustion they could tolerate.

But today, the world has awakened to a truth we can no longer ignore:

A tired mind cannot create.

A stressed mind cannot innovate.

A burned-out mind cannot lead.

Mental health is not a "personal issue."

It is a performance issue.

A business issue.

A leadership issue.

A family issue.

A national issue.

In the modern world, mental wellness is one of the greatest competitive advantages any individual or organization can possess.

This chapter explores why.

THE OLD MODEL: "TOUGH IT OUT."

Many leaders were raised with a simple philosophy:

- "Suck it up."
- "Push through it."
- "Work harder."
- "Don't complain."
- "Stress is normal."
- "Life is hard; deal with it."

This created strong people—yes.
But it also created silent suffering:

- suppressed emotions
- hidden anxiety
- chronic stress
- insomnia
- exhaustion
- poor communication
- unhealthy coping mechanisms
- burnout disguised as loyalty

This wasn't strength.
It was survival.

THE NEW MODEL: "A HEALTHY MIND PERFORMS BETTER."

Today's most effective leaders, companies, and high performers understand this truth:

Mental clarity outranks mental toughness.

Mental wellness improves:

- decision-making
- creativity
- problem-solving
- emotional intelligence
- leadership presence
- communication
- resilience
- consistency
- focus
- innovation

A healthy mind multiplies productivity.
An unhealthy mind destroys it.

THE GENIUS OF DOING NOTHING

Most of us were raised to believe that doing nothing is laziness, weakness, or a waste of time. I used to believe that too—until I discovered the surprising truth: **there is genius in doing nothing.**

Neuroscientists have found that when the brain is at rest—when we are quiet, bored, or intentionally doing nothing—it enters what researchers call the *default mode network*. In this state, the brain solves problems, processes information, restores clarity, and unlocks creativity far more effectively than when we are busy.

In fact, we live in a world where the average adult attention span is now **eight seconds**—one second less than a goldfish.
We are overstimulated by screens, addicted to multitasking (which isn't real—we simply shift attention rapidly), and drowning in noise.

The result?
We are losing our ability to *think*.

But when we step away from the phone... step away from the screen... step away from the constant demands... something remarkable happens.

Our mind begins to breathe again.

One of my favorite metaphors comes from the Kenny Rogers classic, *The Gambler*. In the song, Kenny is traveling with a seasoned gambler on a slow, quiet, boring summer night. With nothing to distract them, the gambler begins to share a simple but profound life strategy:

**"You've got to know when to hold 'em,
know when to fold 'em,
know when to walk away,
and know when to run."**

Boredom created space...
and space created wisdom.

Brain Rest is not weakness.

Brain Rest is brilliance.

Brain Rest is strategy.

Brain Rest is problem-solving.

Brain Rest is where creativity wakes up.

In a world obsessed with motion, Brain Rest becomes a superpower.

When you allow your mind to slow down, your deepest
ideas rise up.

When you pause, you perceive.

When you stop striving, you finally start solving.

Sometimes, doing nothing is the most productive thing you will do all day.

THE HUMAN BRAIN WAS NOT BUILT FOR CONSTANT PRESSURE

Most people are not failing because they are incapable—
they are failing because they are overwhelmed.

The human brain was not designed for:

- nonstop notifications
- constant multitasking
- 24/7 communication
- social comparison
- digital overload
- back-to-back meetings
- financial stress
- perfection culture

·   "always on" expectations

We are living in a world the brain was not designed for—
and that's why mental health has become the new currency of
performance.

THE COST OF POOR MENTAL HEALTH IN ORGANIZATIONS

Let's be real:

A stressed employee is not productive.
A burned-out manager cannot lead.
A mentally exhausted executive makes costly mistakes.

Poor mental health leads to:

- low creativity
- high turnover
- poor teamwork
- reduced innovation
- communication breakdown
- inconsistent performance
- low morale
- decreased engagement

Companies lose billions annually because employees are
overwhelmed
not because they lack skill,
but because they lack space.

GEN Z AND MILLENNIALS PRIORITIZE MENTAL HEALTH— AND THEY'RE RIGHT

Older generations sometimes say:

"Young people are too emotional."
"They can't handle stress."
"They're too sensitive."

But this perspective misses a critical truth:

They are the first generation refusing to normalize emotional suffering.

They're not weaker.
They're tactical.

They're not less capable.
They're more aware.

They don't want to "push through" stress—
they want to prevent it.

And that mindset is more effective in the long run.

They are not rejecting responsibility—
they are rejecting self-destruction.

This is not fragility.
This is progress.

THE CONNECTION BETWEEN MENTAL HEALTH AND SMART WORK

Smart work requires:

- clarity
- focus
- creativity
- emotional stability
- strategic thinking
- centeredness
- self-awareness

None of these are possible when mental health is ignored.

Hard work tolerates stress.
Smart work manages it.

Hard work suppresses emotions.
Smart work understands them.

Hard work sees rest as weakness.
Smart work sees rest as fuel.

Hard work glorifies exhaustion.
Smart work glorifies excellence.

THE THREE LEVELS OF MENTAL WELLNESS

Mental health is not just about "feeling good."
It is about functioning at your highest capacity.

Here are the three levels leaders must understand:

1. Emotional Stability

This is the foundation.

It includes:

- self-regulation
- awareness of triggers
- emotional resilience
- healthy communication
- calm decision-making

A reactive leader creates chaos.
A stable leader creates progress.

2. Mental Clarity

Clarity is the engine of peak performance.

It includes:

- focus
- strategic thinking
- creativity
- innovation
- decisiveness

Clarity turns complexity into simplicity.
Clarity transforms pressure into purpose.

3. Mental Energy

Mental energy is your ability to perform consistently.

It includes:

- sleep
- rest
- recovery
- healthy routines
- proper boundaries

Mental energy is not a luxury—
it is a leadership necessity.

A drained mind cannot produce inspired results.

HOW LEADERS CAN CREATE MENTALLY HEALTHY CULTURES

Leaders must shift from managing people to understanding them.

Here's how:

1. **Reduce unnecessary stress.**
   Remove outdated systems, needless meetings, and unrealistic expectations.

2. **Normalize healthy boundaries.**
   Empower people to disconnect, rest, and recharge.

3. **Value clarity over chaos.**
   Confusion is the enemy of productivity.

4. **Encourage open communication.**
    Psychological safety fuels engagement.

5. **Replace fear-based leadership with inspiration.**
    People perform better when motivated, not threatened.

6. **Model balance at the top.**
    Culture mirrors leadership.

7. **Treat people like humans, not machines.**
    Human beings require energy, rest, and care.

Mental health is not a trend—
it is the foundation of sustainable excellence.

THE FUTURE BELONGS TO EMOTIONALLY INTELLIGENT LEADERS

The leaders who thrive in the modern world will not be:

- the toughest
- the loudest
- the most aggressive
- the most demanding
- They will be:
- emotionally intelligent
- self-aware
- adaptive
- empathetic
- mentally stable
- clear-thinking
- innovative

These leaders will create environments where people feel safe, seen, supported, and inspired—
and in those environments, performance skyrockets.

The younger generation isn't soft.
They're signaling what the future requires.

And the leaders who listen will dominate the next era of work.

CHAPTER EIGHT

THE POWER OF THOUGHT, FOCUS, AND INTENTION

Every great achievement begins long before action.
Long before effort.
Long before execution.

It begins in the mind.

Your thoughts shape your direction.
Your focus shapes your progress.
Your intention shapes your outcomes.

If your mind is scattered, your life becomes scattered.
If your mind is centered, your life becomes powerful.

You cannot build a victorious life with a defeated mindset.
You cannot produce clarity through confusion.
You cannot create extraordinary results with average thinking.

True Success—especially *Success Reimagined*—begins internally.

Let's go deeper.

THE WORLD IS NOT DRIVEN BY MUSCLE— IT IS DRIVEN BY MINDSET

In the industrial age, muscle mattered.
In the information age, mindset matters.

Your most valuable asset is not what you own, what you do, or even what you know—
it is how you think.

The difference between people who rise and people who remain stuck is not talent.
It is not opportunity.
It is not background.
It is not resources.

It is mindset.

Winners think differently.
Leaders think differently.
Innovators think differently.
Creators think differently.
The younger generation thinks differently—and this is why they challenge old systems.

The greatest tool in your entire life is not your job, your business, or your education.

It is your mind.

THOUGHTS ARE NOT HARMLESS—THEY ARE CREATIVE

Most people underestimate the power of thought.

Thoughts are not passive.
They are not background noise.
They are not neutral.

Thoughts are creative forces.

Every thought is building something:
your confidence or your fear,
your clarity or your confusion,
your hope or your hopelessness.

Your mind is always constructing the future you walk into.

What you repeatedly think about eventually shapes:

- Your decisions
- Your behavior
- Your habits
- Your identity
- Your opportunities
- Your limitations
- Your direction
- Your destiny

You cannot think small and live big.
You cannot think defeat and walk in victory.
You cannot think fear and expect courage to appear.

The mind is the soil of your life.
Whatever you plant grows.

FOCUS IS A SUPERPOWER OF THE MODERN AGE

In a world of distractions, the most powerful person is the one who can focus.

We are living in the most distraction-filled era in human history:

- smartphones
- social media
- constant notifications
- endless entertainment
- information overload
- comparison culture
- digital dependency

These distractions don't just waste time—
they break attention into tiny fragments until your mind becomes too scattered to produce meaningful outcomes.

The ability to focus is now a competitive advantage.

Focus allows you to:

- finish what others start
- stay consistent when others quit
- build momentum, others can't see
- think deeply when others skim
- create while others consume

- rise while others remain busy
- Focus is the foundation of mastery.

When you can control your attention, you can control your direction.

INTENTION IS THE DIFFERENCE BETWEEN MOVEMENT AND MOMENTUM

Many people move—but very few move with intention.

Movement is activity.
Intention is purpose.

Movement looks like productivity, but often leads nowhere.
Intention looks quiet, but it builds empires.

To move with intention is to know:

- why you're doing something
- what outcome you want
- what matters most
- what does not matter at all
- what deserves your energy
- what must be eliminated

Action without intention is chaos.
Action with intention is power.

Winners don't leave their direction to chance.
They decide.
They define.

They design.
They direct their energy with precision.

THE FORMULA: THOUGHT → FOCUS → INTENTION → EXECUTION

Let's simplify success in one flow:

1. Thought

You think it.
You create the idea.
You define the possibility.

2. Focus

You aim your attention.
You cut out distractions.
You choose what truly matters.

3. Intention

You align your actions with purpose.
You move deliberately.
You operate with clarity.

4. Execution

This is where work becomes powerful.
Your actions are now fueled by a focused, intentional mind.

This is the foundation of smart work.
This is how consistent people elevate.
This is how average people rise.
This is how leaders separate themselves from the crowd.

THE YOUNGER GENERATION INTUITIVELY UNDERSTANDS THIS

Older generations were taught to work harder.
Younger generations were raised to work smarter.

They understand that:

· attention is currency
· creativity is power
· intention is direction
· clarity is strength
· mental discipline is leadership
· the mind drives everything

They do not want to be busy—
they want to be effective.

They do not want motion—
they want momentum.

They do not want tasks—
they want purpose.

This is why they value mental health, personal growth, creativity, flexibility, and autonomy.

They know productivity begins in the mind—
not in the muscles.

HOW TO STRENGTHEN YOUR MIND FOR HIGH PERFORMANCE

Here are practical steps leaders, parents, professionals, and entrepreneurs can use immediately:

1. Master your mornings.

Your first hour sets your energy, clarity, and direction.

2. Protect your focus ruthlessly.

Increase deep work.
Reduce shallow work.

3. Remove digital clutter.

Turn off notifications.
Limit distractions.
Create digital boundaries.

4. Feed your mind.

Read.
Listen.
Learn.
Study.
Evolve.

5. Think on paper.

Clarity increases when thoughts become visible.

6. Ask powerful questions.

Your mind follows the questions you ask:

- What matters most today?
- What can I eliminate?
- What is the best use of my energy?
- What is the real priority?
- What does victory look like today?

7. Visualize outcomes.

If you cannot see it, you cannot achieve it.

8. Set intentional objectives.

Not vague desires—intentional objectives with meaning, purpose, and alignment.

9. Create focus blocks.

Protect deep concentration like your life depends on it—because your future does.

10. Guard your environment.

Your surroundings shape your thinking.
Your thinking shapes your results.

THE MIND IS YOUR FIRST WORKSPACE

Before you send an email, make a call, launch a business, build a team, or take a risk—
the first work must happen inside your mind.

If your thoughts are aligned, your steps become powerful.
If your focus is aligned, your progress becomes unstoppable.
If your intention is aligned, your outcomes become inevitable.

Success Reimagined begins internally.
Victory is born in the mind long before it appears in your life.

And when you master your thoughts, focus, and intention—
you master yourself.

CHAPTER NINE

WHY PLAY, FREEDOM, AND CREATIVITY FUEL HIGH PERFORMANCE

For decades, society conditioned us to believe that success must be serious...

that work must be heavy...

that productivity must feel painful...

that pressure is the price of progress.

But as we enter a new era of business, leadership, and human potential, a radical truth is emerging:

People perform better when they feel free.

They innovate when they feel safe.

They create when they feel inspired.

They excel when they feel alive.

Play, freedom, and creativity are not luxuries.

They are not childish.

They are not distractions.

They are performance multipliers.

Let's explore why.

THE SCIENCE OF PLAY AND PERFORMANCE

Neuroscience reveals something extraordinary:
When humans experience lightness, curiosity, or joy—the brain
becomes more powerful.

Play activates:

- creativity
- problem-solving
- pattern recognition
- memory
- emotional resilience
- stress reduction
- innovation pathways
- motivation
- energy
- Play is the birthplace of creativity.

Children do it naturally.
Adults unlearn it—and pay the price.

When you lose the ability to play, you lose:

- imagination
- intuition
- fresh ideas
- mental agility
- courage

- perspective
- innovation capacity

Play is not the opposite of productivity.
Play is the engine of it.

FREEDOM IS THE OXYGEN OF HIGH PERFORMANCE

People flourish when they feel free.

Freedom gives you:

- the courage to explore
- the space to think
- the safety to experiment
- the confidence to innovate
- the energy to grow
- the autonomy to lead
- the clarity to create

You cannot unlock genius in an environment of fear.
You cannot unlock excellence through micromanagement.
You cannot unlock innovation under suffocating control.

This is why the younger generation demands flexibility, autonomy, and mental space.

They are not being rebellious.
They are revealing what the human spirit requires to perform
at its best.

CREATIVITY IS THE NEW WORKPLACE SUPERPOWER

In the past, jobs were about repetition.
Now, jobs are about creation.

Automation has taken over repetitive tasks.
AI has taken over data-heavy tasks.
Technology has replaced mechanical tasks.

What remains?

Human creativity.

Creativity is now the most valuable skill in almost every industry:

- Leadership
- Entrepreneurship
- Marketing
- Technology
- Finance
- Government
- Education
- Design
- Strategy
- Innovation
- Problem-solving

Creativity is not artistic—
creativity is visionary.

It is the ability to:

- connect ideas

- see patterns
- ask new questions
- imagine new solutions
- disrupt old systems
- elevate stagnant environments
- Creativity multiplies value.

Hard work adds.
Smart work multiplies.
Creativity transforms.

WHY MOST ADULTS LOSE THEIR CREATIVITY

Somewhere between childhood and adulthood, many people lose their creative edge.
Why?

Because creativity is crushed under:

- stress
- fear of failure
- perfectionism
- pressure
- judgment
- harsh criticism
- rigid systems
- outdated models
- environments that punish mistakes
- leaders who suppress ideas
- cultures that value obedience over innovation

· Creativity cannot exist where fear dominates.

Children create naturally because they feel free.
Adults stop creating because they feel constrained.

The return to creativity is the return to power.

THE YOUNGER GENERATION IS WIRED FOR CREATIVE WORK

This is one of the greatest misunderstandings between generations:

Older generations were shaped by systems.
Younger generations were shaped by possibilities.

Older generations were trained to follow.
Younger generations were trained to explore.

Older generations learned stability.
Younger generations learned adaptability.

This is why they value:

· flexible work
· creative problem-solving
· autonomy
· innovation
· playfulness
· collaborative environments
· digital expression
· meaningful work

They don't want to follow outdated rules.
They want to create new ones.

They are not disobedient.
They are creative.

They are not unfocused.
They are exploratory.

They are not lazy.
They are intentionally seeking environments where their potential can thrive.

PLAY CREATES THE CONDITIONS FOR GENIUS

Some of the most world-changing ideas were born in environments of play:

- Steve Jobs walking barefoot through orchards
- Einstein imagining himself riding on beams of light
- Walt Disney sketching cartoons instead of studying
- Richard Branson brainstorming on islands

Google encouraging employees to spend 20% of their time tinkering

Pixar designing offices that feel like playgrounds

Play is not unprofessional.
Play is strategic.

When your mind is relaxed, it shifts into creative mode, allowing breakthrough ideas to flow.

Play reduces fear.
Fear blocks innovation.

Play reduces stress.
Stress destroys creativity.

Play opens the imagination.
Imagination opens the future.

FREEDOM IS THE FOUNDATION OF INNOVATION

People innovate when they feel:

- trusted
- valued
- respected
- empowered
- safe

Freedom multiplies:

- initiative
- ownership
- courage
- problem-solving
- engagement
- loyalty
- excellence

Freedom doesn't make people irresponsible—
it makes them powerful.

The best leaders don't tighten control.
They widen trust.

The best parents don't restrict potential.
They release it.

The best companies don't command innovation.
They create space for it.

HOW LEADERS CAN CULTIVATE PLAY, FREEDOM & CREATIVITY

You can create environments where performance soars by implementing a few simple practices:

1. Encourage idea generation.

Ask:
"What else is possible?"
"What are we missing?"
"WhAt would you try if failure was not a risk?"

2. Celebrate experimentation.

Make it safe to try, test, and learn.

3. Replace rigid rules with flexible frameworks.

Structure should support creativity—not suffocate it.

4. Create environments with visual inspiration.

Bright spaces spark bright ideas.

5. Allow autonomy in work methods.

People perform best when trusted to choose how they work.

6. Protect creative time.

Deep work sessions
No-meeting days
Focus blocks
Innovation hours

7. Encourage playfulness.

Humor.
Movement.
Breaks.
Brainstorming games.
Vision-building sessions.

Small sparks ignite big breakthroughs.

8. Eliminate fear-based leadership.

Fear kills creativity faster than failure ever will.

9. Empower collaboration instead of competition.

Creative energy multiplies when people combine strengths.

10. Model freedom at the top.

Leaders set the psychological tone of an organization.
If leaders are rigid, teams shrink.
If leaders are expansive, teams rise.

PLAY, FREEDOM & CREATIVITY ARE THE FUTURE OF WORK

The world is shifting from mechanical labor to mental mastery.

The old formula:
Work harder → Get ahead

The new formula:
Think deeper → Create more → Contribute greater → Win bigger

Play unlocks imagination.
Freedom unlocks courage.
Creativity unlocks possibility.

This is not a trend.
This is evolution.

The companies that embrace this will dominate their industries.
The families that embrace this will raise innovators.
The leaders that embrace this will shape the future.
The individuals that embrace this will live fulfilled, impactful, victorious lives.

Because success is no longer about force.

True Success is about flow.

THE NEW WORK BLUEPRINT

CHAPTER TEN

THE SMART WORK MATRIX (SIMPLIFIED FOR LEADERS)

Every generation discovers a new way of working that shapes its destiny.

In the agricultural age, strength mattered.
In the industrial age, repetition mattered.
In the information age, knowledge mattered.
In the digital age, speed and creativity matter.

And now, entering the smart age, one thing matters more than anything else:

Your ability to work in alignment with who you are and what produces the highest impact.

This is the foundation of the Smart Work Matrix—
a simple, powerful framework that helps leaders, professionals, CEOs, and organizations identify how people should work for maximum effectiveness, minimum stress, and optimal performance.

We must prepare the world for this concept. In this chapter, we simplify the matrix so every reader—from parents to business leaders—can apply it instantly.

THE PURPOSE OF THE SMART WORK MATRIX

The Smart Work Matrix exists for one reason:

To move people from exhaustion to excellence
by helping them work in their natural zone of strength.

You cannot build a victorious life or a high-performing team if people are trapped in the wrong zone.

Leaders fail when they force people into roles that drain them.
Parents struggle when they pressure their children into paths that don't fit them.
Companies collapse when they reward busyness over effectiveness.

The Smart Work Matrix solves this.

It identifies exactly where a person performs best so they can create more value, more impact, more fulfillment—with less stress.

THE FOUR ZONES OF THE SMART WORK MATRIX

Zone 1: Your Genius Zone

Zone 2: Your Growth Zone

Zone 3: Your Grind Zone

Zone 4: Your Give-Up Zone

Let's break down each one.

ZONE 1—YOUR GENIUS ZONE

Where you are strongest.
Where you excel effortlessly.
Where your value multiplies.

Your Genius Zone is where:

· You feel energized
· You perform naturally
· You solve problems easily
· You produce extraordinary results
· You contribute the highest value
· You enter a "flow state."
· Time passes quickly
· creativity comes alive.

Your Genius Zone is your highest contribution to the world. It's where talent meets passion and produces impact.

Leaders who operate in their Genius Zone outperform those who grind in their weakness.

Examples:

- A CEO who is a visionary, not an operations manager
- A child who thinks visually, not verbally
- A sales leader who thrives in relationships, not spreadsheets
- An employee who excels in strategy, not paperwork

When you work in your Genius Zone, your effort decreases but your impact increases.

This is smart work at its peak.

ZONE 2—YOUR GROWTH ZONE

Where you develop new strengths.
Where learning produces momentum.
Where effort leads to mastery.

Your Growth Zone is where:

- You stretch
- You learn
- You adapt
- You build new skills
- You overcome challenges
- You increase capacity
- This zone strengthens your future Genius Zone.

Even high performers spend time here because growth is essential for leadership evolution.

Examples:

- Public speaking if you're great at communication but inexperienced on stage.
- Learning new technology that enhances your profession
- Improving leadership skills as you rise in your organization

Growth is not always comfortable—but it is powerful.

ZONE 3—YOUR GRIND ZONE

Where work feels difficult.
Where results require enormous effort.
Where stress increases, and creativity decreases.

Your Grind Zone is where:

- work feels forced
- tasks are draining
- motivation is low
- frustration builds
- energy drops
- performance is inconsistent

The Grind Zone is not bad in small doses—
sometimes life requires it.

But living here long-term leads to:

- burnout
- anxiety
- resentment
- disengagement

- decline in quality
- loss of motivation

This is the zone where many workers, parents, and leaders get stuck—because they think grinding equals loyalty.

Grinding is not loyalty.
Grinding is misalignment.

ZONE 4—YOUR GIVE-UP ZONE

Where you do not belong.
Where you are not competent.
Where you add no value.
Where failure is guaranteed.

Your Give-Up Zone is where:

- You consistently struggle
- You cannot progress
- skills are missing
- interest is absent
- frustration is high
- potential is zero
- productivity collapses
- This is the zone of complete misfit.

People in this zone are not lazy—
they are misplaced.

A visionary forced into detailed spreadsheets lives here.
A creative forced into rigid rules lives here.
A relational person forced into isolation lives here.

The Give-Up Zone destroys confidence and triggers self-doubt, even in highly capable people.

WHY LEADERS MUST UNDERSTAND THE MATRIX

The greatest mistake leaders make is forcing people to perform in their Grind and Give-Up zones.

The smartest leaders—the ones who build world-class teams and cultures—do this instead:

1. **Identify strengths**
   They understand the natural wiring of their team.

2. **Assign roles strategically**
   They match people to zones, not titles.

3. **Remove people from draining tasks**
   They eliminate energy-draining work that kills performance.

4. **Build systems to support weaknesses**
   Instead of forcing people to fix everything, they compensate through collaboration and tools.

5. **Maximize genius, minimize grind**
   They optimize every person's highest contribution.

This is how companies improve culture, performance, retention, and innovation.

This is how families raise confident children.

This is how individuals elevate their careers.

This is the essence of smart leadership.

THE SMART WORK MATRIX FOR THE MODERN WORKFORCE

The younger generation intuitively understands this concept.

They refuse to:

- stay in roles that drain them
- buy into "just suffer through it"
- live in work that kills their joy
- commit to careers misaligned with their identity
- grind endlessly with no growth

They want:

- to work in their strengths
- to innovate
- to feel alive
- to build something meaningful
- to become the best version of themselves

They don't fear work.
They fear wasted potential.

They don't avoid effort.
They avoid misalignment.

They don't give up easily.
They give up on the wrong paths.

This is insight, not weakness.

HOW TO APPLY THE SMART WORK MATRIX IMMEDIATELY

Here are practical steps for leaders, parents, CEOs, and professionals:

1. Identify your Genius Zone

Ask yourself:

- What energizes me?
- What do I do better than most?
- What feels natural?
- What produces high impact with less effort?

2. Protect your Genius Zone

Schedule it.
Prioritize it.
Guard it.
Build systems around it.

3. Expand your Growth Zone

Learn skills that support your Genius Zone and improve your leadership capacity.

4. Reduce your Grind Zone

Use tools, automation, delegation, or collaboration to minimize Grind tasks.

5. Eliminate your Give-Up Zone

Stop forcing yourself (or your team) into work that does not match natural wiring.

6. Build teams around the Matrix

Every strong team needs multiple Genius Zones working together.

Leaders don't build teams of identical strengths.
They build teams of compatible strengths.

WHEN PEOPLE WORK IN THEIR GENIUS ZONE, THEY BECOME UNSTOPPABLE

The world doesn't need more exhausted workers.
It needs more aligned workers.
It needs more inspired leaders.
It needs more people operating in their full potential.

The Smart Work Matrix is the blueprint.
It is how individuals rise.
It is how organizations thrive.
It is how nations develop.
It is how the future is built.

Smart work is not about doing less—
it is about doing what matters most.

When you find your zone, you find your power.

CHAPTER ELEVEN

TEN PRINCIPLES FOR A HIGH-PERFORMANCE LIFE

High performance is not accidental.
It is not reserved for the gifted, the privileged, or the lucky.
It is the result of intentional choices, repeated daily, that shape a life of clarity, power, and impact.

Most people fail not because they lack talent...
but because they lack principles.

Principles give structure to your potential.
They turn energy into excellence.
They transform motion into momentum.
They create consistency, direction, and purpose.

In this chapter, we explore ten principles that will help any individual—CEO, parent, professional, entrepreneur, or government leader—live a life of productivity, fulfillment, and sustainable success.

Let's begin.

PRINCIPLE 1—CLARITY OVER CONFUSION

Confusion kills more dreams than failure ever will.

Most people don't know:

- what they want
- why they want it
- what matters most
- what they should eliminate
- what direction they should take
- Clarity is the master skill of high performance.
- When you are clear:
- Your decisions become simple
- Your thinking becomes sharp
- Your focus becomes powerful
- Your results become predictable

People fail because they chase too many things.
Winners succeed because they focus on one thing at a time.

Clarity is your compass.

PRINCIPLE 2—ENERGY OVER TIME

You don't need more time.
You need more energy.

What good is eight hours of work if you accomplish nothing?
What good is a long day if your mind is scattered?

Your energy—physical, emotional, mental, and creative—determines the quality of your output.

Protect your energy:

- Rest intentionally
- Recover deliberately
- Exercise consistently
- Eat for performance
- Minimize stress
- Guard your environment

Time is limited.
Energy can be multiplied.

High performers manage their energy, not their hours.

PRINCIPLE 3—FOCUS OVER DISTRACTION

The modern world is designed to break your attention: notifications, messages, comparison, scrolling, noise.

A distracted mind cannot create brilliance.

High performers eliminate distractions aggressively.

They know:

- multitasking is the enemy
- deep work produces exceptional results
- focus compounds in value
- concentration separates leaders from followers

Your future depends on your ability to focus on what matters most—and ignore everything else.

Focus turns average people into extraordinary performers.

PRINCIPLE 4—ALIGNMENT OVER FORCE

You should not have to force your life into existence.

Force exhausts you.
Alignment elevates you.

When your work aligns with:

- Your strengths
- Your passions
- Your personality
- Your natural gifts
- Your deeper purpose
- You become unstoppable.

Alignment makes effort feel lighter.
It is the foundation of the Smart Work philosophy.

When you operate in your Genius Zone, true success feels natural.

PRINCIPLE 5—SYSTEMS OVER WILLPOWER

Willpower is unreliable.
Systems are undefeated.

Most people depend on motivation.
High performers depend on structure.

Systems create:

- consistency
- reliability
- predictability
- discipline
- flow
- freedom

A system turns difficult tasks into effortless habits.

A system turns goals into outcomes.

Systems transform who you are into who you are becoming.

PRINCIPLE 6—GROWTH OVER COMFORT

Comfort feels good, but it kills potential.
Growth feels uncomfortable, but it unlocks greatness.

Every major breakthrough in your life will require discomfort:

- learning something new
- facing fears
- letting go of old patterns

- developing new skills
- entering unfamiliar environments

Growth expands your capacity.
It increases your confidence.
It elevates your value.

High performers do not avoid discomfort—
they embrace it.

PRINCIPLE 7—CONSISTENCY OVER INTENSITY

Intensity is exciting, but it is temporary.
Consistency is boring, but it is transformational.

Anyone can work hard for a day.
High performers work smart every day.

Consistency builds:

- habits
- momentum
- excellence
- reputation
- mastery
- trust

Small, consistent actions outperform big, inconsistent bursts of effort.

Consistency wins every time.

PRINCIPLE 8—CREATIVITY OVER PERFECTION

Perfection kills progress.

Many talented people never share their ideas or start their dreams because they fear:

- mistakes
- criticism
- looking unqualified
- not being perfect

But high performers know:

Creativity is more valuable than perfection.

Creativity produces solutions.
Perfection produces paralysis.

Innovation requires taking risks.
Perfection requires staying safe.

Creativity moves you forward.
Perfection holds you back.

PRINCIPLE 9—CONTRIBUTION OVER COMPETITION

Competition divides.
Contribution multiplies.

You rise higher when you help others rise.
You grow faster when you share your strengths.
You build influence when you contribute value.

High performers are not concerned with being the best in the room.
They are concerned with making the room better.

Contribution creates:

- loyalty
- opportunity
- impact
- legacy

You do not need to compete with others—
you need to compete with who you were yesterday.

PRINCIPLE 10—VICTORY OVER SUCCESS

Success is external.
Victory is internal.

Success is measured by:

- money
- status
- fame
- applause

Victory is measured by:

- fulfillment
- authenticity
- freedom

- purpose
- impact

Success can be taken away.
Victory is who you become.

High performers do not chase success.
They pursue victory—and true success follows them.

A HIGH-PERFORMANCE LIFE IS BUILT, NOT BORN

Every principle in this chapter is a choice:

- clarity
- energy
- focus
- alignment
- systems
- growth
- consistency
- creativity
- contribution
- victory

When you master these principles, your life elevates.
Your work becomes meaningful.
Your leadership becomes powerful.
Your impact becomes inevitable.

High performance is not about working harder.

It is about living intentionally.

Thinking clearly.

Acting purposefully.

And rising consistently.

These principles create winners—in business, in leadership, in family, in life.

This is *Success Reimagined*.

CHAPTER TWELVE

THE FUTURE OF WORK: WHAT THE NEXT GENERATION ALREADY UNDERSTANDS

The world is shifting faster than ever.
Industries are evolving.
Technology is accelerating.
Human expectations are transforming.
Entire career paths are disappearing—while new ones emerge overnight.

But in the middle of this rapid transformation, one truth has become unmistakable:

The younger generation is not confused about the future of work.
They already understand it.
It's the older systems that are behind.

This chapter explores what the next generation sees clearly—and what leaders must embrace if they want to stay relevant, attract high-level talent, and build organizations that thrive in the new era.

THE FUTURE OF WORK IS NOT ABOUT WORK— IT'S ABOUT VALUE

For decades, work was measured by:

- hours
- effort
- attendance
- obedience
- longevity
- position
- schedule

But the world now measures value, not volume.

The younger generation understands that:

- Impact matters more than hours.
- Skill matters more than titles.
- Results matter more than routines.
- Creativity matters more than compliance.
- Purpose matters more than position.

They are not rejecting work.
They are demanding work that produces value—not just movement.

This shift is not laziness.
It is progress.

THE FUTURE OF WORK IS FLEXIBLE, NOT FIXED

The younger generation rejects outdated rules like:

- "You must be in the office."
- "You must work these exact hours."
- "You must sit at this desk."
- "You must follow this rigid routine."

They value flexibility because flexibility fuels:

- creativity
- problem-solving
- mental health
- autonomy
- productivity
- work-life balance

They know you produce better work when you're:

- energized
- inspired
- mentally clear
- physically comfortable
- emotionally stable

Flexibility does not reduce performance—
it enhances it.

Organizations that understand this will attract the best talent.
Organizations that resist will lose them.

THE FUTURE OF WORK IS DIGITAL-FIRST

Young people know the world through:

- technology
- apps
- digital communication
- online collaboration
- automation tools
- AI
- remote solutions
- global platforms

They do not separate physical work from digital work—
to them, it's all one integrated system.

The older generation views technology as a tool.
The younger generation views technology as an environment.

This gives them enormous advantages:

- faster learning
- easier adaptation
- quicker execution
- broader perspective
- global awareness
- creative solutions

They are building the future because they are already living in it.

THE FUTURE OF WORK VALUES WELL-BEING OVER WEARINESS

Burnout culture is dead—and for good reason.

The younger generation understands something profound:

A healthy mind creates better results than a tired one.

This is why they value:

- mental health
- rest
- meaningful work
- autonomy
- environments that feel human
- cultures where they are seen and valued
- leaders who inspire rather than pressure

They are not rejecting responsibility—
they are rejecting self-destruction.

They want to thrive, not survive.
They want to grow, not grind.

And any organization that supports this will rise with them.

THE FUTURE OF WORK REWARDS CREATIVITY, NOT COMPLIANCE

Compliance was the old requirement.
Creativity is the new superpower.

The younger generation sees:

- problems differently
- systems differently
- possibilities differently
- limitations differently
- solutions differently

They don't want to follow instructions—
they want to improve them.

They don't want to repeat processes—
they want to transform them.

They don't want to do work—
they want to create value.

This is why leaders must shift from:

- commanding → inspiring
- controlling → empowering
- micromanaging → trusting
- dictating → collaborating
- repeating → innovating
- Creativity is the new currency of progress.

THE FUTURE OF WORK IS GLOBAL, NOT LOCAL

Young people think globally because their lives are global.

They collaborate with people:

- across time zones
- across countries
- across cultures
- across digital platforms

They see opportunity everywhere, not just in their local geography.

This global mindset:

- increases adaptability
- expands perspective
- multiplies innovation
- elevates competitiveness
- accelerates learning

Organizations that embrace global thinking will dominate the future marketplace.
Those that stay local will become obsolete.

THE FUTURE OF WORK IS PURPOSE-DRIVEN

More than any generation before them, young people seek meaning.

They want work that:

- aligns with their identity
- reflects their values
- impacts the world
- contributes to something greater
- allows them to express their potential
- connects them to a mission
- Purpose fuels performance.

When people feel part of something meaningful, they:

- work diligently
- stay longer
- innovate more
- commit deeper
- grow faster
- contribute greater

Purpose is not sentimental.
Purpose is strategic.

THE FUTURE OF WORK IS BUILT ON CHOICE, NOT EXPECTATION

Older generations followed a script:

- go to school
- get a degree
- get a job
- stay loyal
- retire tired

The younger generation rejects this script entirely.

- They know they have options:
- entrepreneurship
- digital careers
- remote work
- multiple income streams
- freelance economy
- global opportunities
- online businesses
- creative industries

Choice creates empowerment.
Empowerment creates confidence.
Confidence creates innovation.

This is why the next generation innovates faster:

They do not feel trapped—
they feel free.

THE FUTURE OF WORK IS BUILT ON IDENTITY, NOT INDUSTRY

Industries collapse.
Titles disappear.
Jobs evolve.
Markets shift.

But identity remains.

The younger generation focuses on:

- who they are
- what they do best
- how they are wired
- what they care about
- what aligns with their gifts

They seek careers aligned with their Genius Zone—
not careers chosen for them.

And this makes them more adaptable, more strategic, and more resilient.

THE FUTURE OF WORK BELONGS TO THOSE WHO THINK DIFFERENTLY

Not to those who:

- follow arbitrary rules
- stay busy
- grind endlessly
- repeat the past

But to those who:

- challenge old definitions
- think independently
- embrace creativity
- work in alignment
- prioritize mental health
- value purpose
- innovate boldly
- lead with emotional intelligence
- use technology wisely
- operate in their Genius Zone

The younger generation is not the problem.
They are the preview.

They are not unmotivated.
They are awakened.

They are not rejecting work.
They are redefining it.

And the leaders who embrace their worldview will shape the next era of progress.

Because the future of work is not coming.

It is already here.
And the younger generation is already standing in it.

SECTION V

FOR LEADERS

CHAPTER THIRTEEN

WHAT EVERY CEO NEEDS TO KNOW ABOUT TALENT TODAY

The greatest challenge for today's leaders is not technology. It's not competition.

It's not market volatility.

It's not even economic unpredictability.

The greatest challenge—and the greatest opportunity—is talent.

Talent has become the most valuable resource on earth.

Not oil.

Not data.

Not real estate.

Not capital.

Talent.

The people.

The thinkers.

The creators.

The innovators.

The contributors who can elevate an organization from average to unstoppable.

But here's the truth many CEOs have not yet accepted:

Talent is evolving faster than leadership.

To lead today's workforce—and tomorrow's—CEOs must understand the new psychology, new priorities, and new expectations of modern talent.

This chapter is your blueprint.

THE OLD TALENT MODEL HAS COLLAPSED

The old rules of leadership said:

- "Give them a salary and they'll stay."
- "Give them a title and they'll follow."
- "Give them a desk and they'll perform."
- "Give them instructions and they'll obey."
- "Give them pressure and they'll produce."
- "Give them benefits and they'll be loyal."

Those days are over.

Today's workforce is not motivated by pressure—they are motivated by purpose.
They are not loyal to positions—they are loyal to people.
They don't care about titles—they care about impact.

The talent landscape has changed.
And CEOs who don't adapt will lose their best people to leaders
who understand the shift.

THE NEW TALENT ECONOMY: WHAT PEOPLE WANT NOW

Modern talent wants five things—and CEOs must deliver them to
attract, keep, and elevate high performers.

1. Meaningful Work

People no longer want to simply "do tasks."
They want to contribute.

They ask:

- "Does this matter?"
- "Does this align with who I am?"
- "Am I making a difference?"

When people feel their work is meaningful, they give more than
effort—they give passion.

2. Growth Opportunities

Today's workforce wants:

- training
- mentorship
- advancement
- new skills
- leadership development

They don't want to stagnate.
They want to evolve.

If your organization doesn't offer growth, your top people will leave for one that does.

3. Flexibility and Autonomy

This is non-negotiable.

People want:

- freedom in how they work
- freedom in where they work
- freedom in when they work

Flexibility increases:

- productivity
- creativity
- loyalty
- engagement
- retention

Autonomy is not a risk—
it is a recruitment and retention superpower.

4. Healthy Culture

People will leave a toxic environment even if it pays well.

They want:

- psychological safety
- trust

- respect
- open communication
- collaboration
- humane leadership

A great culture turns employees into ambassadors.
A bad culture turns them into exit candidates.

5. Purposeful Leadership

Today's workforce values leaders who are:

- empathetic
- authentic
- visionary
- emotionally intelligent
- supportive
- transparent

People don't quit companies—
they quit leaders.

They don't leave because of workload—
they leave because of how they're treated.

Leadership is the #1 predictor of retention.

THE CEO WHO WILL WIN THE FUTURE OF WORK

The CEOs who thrive in the next decade will not be the ones who demand more—
but the ones who understand more.

They will be:

- emotionally intelligent
- mentally agile
- purpose-driven
- flexible
- innovative
- people-centered
- creative
- intuitive
- empowering

These leaders will:

- attract top talent organically
- keep people engaged
- inspire loyalty
- build high-performance cultures
- innovate faster
- adapt stronger
- grow consistently

The CEO of the future is not a commander—
they are a conductor.

They orchestrate strengths.
They elevate people.
They create environments where talent thrives.

THE NEW TALENT FORMULA

The world's most successful organizations follow one core formula for talent:

Hire for potential.
Train for skill.
Lead for humanity.
Reward for impact.
Promote for alignment.

This formula transforms organizations.

THE MILLENNIAL, GEN Z & GEN ALPHA TALENT MINDSET

Understanding the younger workforce is essential.
Here's what CEOs must know:

- They value meaning, not meaningless work.
- They seek growth, not stagnation.
- They demand flexibility, not rigid rules.
- They crave leaders, not bosses.
- They prioritize mental health, not burnout.
- They want opportunity, not obligation.

- They choose alignment, not tradition.
- They follow purpose, not pressure.

This mindset doesn't make them entitled—
it makes them evolved.

THE CRITICAL MISTAKE CEOS MAKE

Many CEOs misinterpret the younger generation's standards as:

- laziness
- disloyalty
- entitlement
- rebellion
- lack of work ethic

But this generation is the most entrepreneurial, informed, creative, and adaptable group in modern history.

They don't want to avoid work—
they want to avoid meaningless work.

They don't want easy jobs—
they want impactful jobs.

They don't want comfort—
they want purpose.

They don't want benefits—
they want better ways of working.

This is not entitlement.
This is enlightenment.

HOW CEOS CAN ATTRACT AND RETAIN TOP TALENT TODAY

Here are the leadership practices that define world-class organizations:

1. **Build a culture of trust**
   Micromanagement kills talent.
   Trust multiplies it.

2. **Focus on strengths, not weaknesses**
   Use the Smart Work Matrix to place people where they thrive.

3. **Create pathways for advancement**
   Clear growth = long-term loyalty.

4. **Give meaningful autonomy**
   Freedom fuels innovation.

5. **Communicate with clarity and empathy**
   People crave understanding and direction.

6. **Prioritize mental health and well-being**
   Healthy employees outperform exhausted ones.

7. **Reward contribution, not conformity**
   Recognize results, not busyness.

8. **Develop leaders, not managers**
   Leaders inspire. Managers instruct.

9. **Cultivate a sense of mission**

Purpose is a magnet for extraordinary people.

10. **Celebrate creativity and initiative**

Great ideas come from unexpected places.

THE CEO WHO UNDERSTANDS TALENT UNDERSTANDS THE FUTURE

Talent is not a workforce to manage—
it is a force to unlock.

Organizations that treat people like numbers will die in the new era of work.
Organizations that treat people like partners will rise.

The CEOs who embrace this chapter will not only lead companies—
they will shape industries, build cultures, and influence nations.

Because the future of work belongs to leaders who understand one powerful truth:

People are not resources.
People are the advantage.

CHAPTER FOURTEEN

WHAT EVERY PARENT NEEDS TO KNOW ABOUT THE NEXT GENERATION

Every generation of parents has looked at the youth and said some version of this:

"Kids these days are different."

But today, those words carry more weight than ever—because this generation is different.

They think differently.
They learn differently.
They work differently.
They communicate differently.
They define success differently.

And most importantly:

They need to be led differently.

Parents are not just raising children anymore—
they are raising innovators, creators, leaders, entrepreneurs, global citizens, and digital natives.

This chapter is a guide for every parent who wants to understand today's emerging generation, empower them, and prepare them for a future that will look nothing like the past.

THE BIGGEST MISUNDERSTANDING BETWEEN PARENTS AND THE YOUNGER GENERATION

Many parents say:

- "They don't want to work."
- "They're too sensitive."
- "They're unfocused."
- "They lack discipline."
- "They're addicted to their phones."
- "They expect everything handed to them."
- "They don't listen."

But here's the truth:

They want to work—
just not the old definition of work.

They want to be disciplined—
just not in meaningless tasks.

They want to focus—
but not on outdated philosophies.

They want to learn—
but not from fear-driven leadership.

They want to be responsible—
but in ways aligned with their identity and purpose.

They are not the problem.
They are the product of a transformed world.

Parents must upgrade the way they understand, communicate with, and lead this generation.

THIS GENERATION IS NOT LAZY—THEY ARE STRATEGIC

This generation wants:

- meaningful work
- flexibility
- mental health
- creativity
- contribution
- purpose
- alignment
- autonomy
- innovation
- impact

They don't want to "work hard" just to survive.
They want to work smart to thrive.

They grew up watching older generations:

- burn out
- sacrifice health
- sacrifice identity
- stay in unfulfilling jobs
- chase success instead of fulfillment
- follow systems that led nowhere

And they are saying:
"There has to be a better way."

This is not laziness—
this is intelligence.

THE NEXT GENERATION VALUES MENTAL HEALTH

This generation is the first to say:

- "Anxiety is not normal."
- "Burnout is not success."
- "I need rest."
- "I need balance."
- "I need clarity."
- "I need emotional safety."

They refuse to normalize suffering—
and that is a sign of awareness, not weakness.

Parents must understand:

You cannot motivate a stressed, overwhelmed, or mentally exhausted child through pressure.

You can only motivate them through:

- support
- understanding
- encouragement
- empathy
- purposeful direction

This generation performs best when they feel their best.

THE NEXT GENERATION VALUES IDENTITY OVER EXPECTATION

Past generations were taught to follow a script:

- Go to school.
- Get a degree.
- Find a job.
- Stay loyal.
- Retire at 65.

But the next generation sees countless paths:

- online business
- digital careers
- entrepreneurship
- freelancing
- remote work

- creative industries
- global collaboration
- multiple income streams

They are not trying to be difficult.
They are trying to find an identity-driven life, not an expectation-driven one.

Parents must understand that their children are not living in the world of the past—
And should not be guided by outdated expectations.

THE NEXT GENERATION LEARNS DIFFERENTLY

They learn through:

- YouTube
- TikTok
- search engines
- online courses
- community learning
- interactive platforms
- global conversations
- They learn quickly, visually, creatively, and socially.

This doesn't mean they lack depth—
it means they have more access to knowledge than any generation before them.

Parents must shift from teaching information.
→ to teaching interpretation, wisdom, and application.

THE NEXT GENERATION COMMUNICATES DIFFERENTLY

They communicate:

- faster
- digitally
- visually
- socially
- collaboratively

Parents often misinterpret this as disrespect or disconnection.

But the truth is:

This generation communicates more than any generation
in history—
just in different ways.

Parents must adapt communication styles that are:

- clear
- encouraging
- conversational
- empathetic
- tech-aware

The goal is not to force them to talk like the past—
but to understand how they talk today.

THE NEXT GENERATION VALUES PURPOSE OVER PRESSURE

In the past, pressure was a motivator.

But this generation responds to:

- meaning
- inspiration
- authenticity
- passion
- clarity
- purpose-driven direction

Pressure may create obedience—
but purpose creates excellence.

Parents must stop trying to push their children.
And start trying to ignite them.

Ignition produces lifelong motivation.

THE NEXT GENERATION THINKS GLOBALLY

They are not limited by:

- geography
- local opportunities
- old traditions
- cultural boundaries
- Their mind is global.

They have:

- global friends
- global exposure
- global perspectives
- global opportunities

Parents must expand their conversations beyond the local world and help their children think bigger, wider, and deeper.

THE NEXT GENERATION NEEDS COACHES, NOT COMMANDERS

Parents are no longer just authority figures.
They must become:

- mentors
- coaches
- guides
- supporters
- listeners
- encouragers.

Authority creates compliance.
Coaching creates competence.

Parents who coach instead of command will raise confident, independent, empowered leaders.

HOW PARENTS CAN LEAD THIS GENERATION EFFECTIVELY

Here are practical ways to connect with, motivate, and empower the next generation:

1. **Listen before you lead.**
   Understand their world before directing their path.

2. **Ask questions instead of giving orders.**
   Questions awaken ownership.

3. **Validate their feelings.**
   Emotional safety creates trust.

4. **Encourage exploration.**
   Let them try, learn, and experiment.

5. **Support their strengths.**
   Place them in their Genius Zone early.

6. **Remove unnecessary pressure.**
   Pressure shuts down potential.

7. **Model healthy habits.**
   Children imitate what they see.

8. **Give responsibility, not just rules.**
   Responsibility develops leadership.

9. **Celebrate progress, not just perfection.**
   Progress builds confidence.

10. **Build relationship, not control.**
    Relationship is the bridge to influence.

THE NEXT GENERATION IS NOT BROKEN—THEY ARE BRILLIANT

They are:

- more creative
- more aware
- more adaptable
- more connected
- more empathetic
- more innovative
- more entrepreneurial

They question the world because they want to improve it.
They challenge systems because they want to elevate them.
They refuse old definitions because they want better ones.

This generation has the potential to transform industries, nations, and the future—
but only if parents understand the gold they're raising.

Great parents don't raise children for the past.
They raise children for the future.

And the future is already here.

CHAPTER FIFTEEN

BUILDING A HIGH-PERFORMANCE CULTURE AT WORK AND AT HOME

C ulture is not an accident.
It is not a vibe.
It is not a slogan.
It is not a mission statement written on a wall.

Culture is created—intentionally or unintentionally—through the daily habits, behaviors, systems, conversations, and expectations that shape how people work, think, and relate.

Every workplace has a culture.
Every home has a culture.
Every team, organization, family, and community has one.

The question is not "Do we have a culture?"
The question is "Is our culture building people—or breaking them?"

In this chapter, we explore how to design environments that produce excellence, wellness, discipline, creativity, and purpose... whether you are leading a company, a team, or a family.

THE POWER OF CULTURE: IT CREATES BEHAVIOR

Culture determines:

- how people act
- how people treat each other
- how people show up
- how conflicts get resolved
- how pressure is handled
- how excellence is defined
- how ideas are shared
- how mistakes are treated
- how leaders lead
- how teams think

Culture is more powerful than strategy.
More influential than instruction.
More defining than rules.

People do not rise to the level of their goals—
they rise to the level of the culture around them.

THE TWO CULTURES THAT DESTROY POTENTIAL

There are two environments that crush potential and suffocate performance:

1. Fear-Based Culture

A culture where people feel:

- insecure
- judged
- criticized
- threatened
- untrusted
- micromanaged
- emotionally unsafe

Fear-based cultures produce:

- high turnover
- poor performance
- low creativity
- resentment
- gossip
- burnout
- compliance, not excellence

Fear kills innovation.
Fear kills confidence.
Fear kills intelligence.
Fear kills initiative.

2. Perfection Culture

A culture where:

- mistakes are punished
- failure is shamed
- expectations are unrealistic
- image matters more than authenticity
- pressure is constant
- nothing is ever good enough

Perfection culture produces:

- anxiety
- paralysis
- dishonesty
- underperformance
- secret struggles
- unhealthy competition
- Perfection destroys people from the inside out.

THE THREE CULTURES THAT BUILD HIGH PERFORMANCE

Now let's explore the opposite—
cultures that elevate people and produce exceptional results.

1. Growth Culture

Where learning is valued more than being right.

This culture encourages:

- curiosity
- feedback
- trial and error
- experimentation
- asking questions
- continuous improvement

People in growth cultures feel:

- safe to try
- safe to fail
- safe to learn
- safe to evolve

This is the foundation of innovation and leadership development.

2. Contribution Culture

Where everyone is expected—and empowered—to add value.

Contribution cultures:

- reward initiative
- celebrate strengths
- encourage collaboration
- eliminate ego-driven competition
- highlight impact
- promote teamwork

People in contribution cultures think:
"How can I help? What can I bring?"

This creates alignment, momentum, and synergy.

3. Well-Being Culture

Where people are treated like humans, not machines.

Well-being cultures prioritize:

- mental health
- rest
- boundaries
- supportive leadership
- emotional intelligence
- clear communication

This environment produces:

- longevity
- loyalty
- consistent performance
- healthy motivation
- sustainable excellence

Well-being fuels high performance.
Exhaustion destroys it.

HOW TO BUILD A HIGH-PERFORMANCE CULTURE AT WORK

Here are practical steps for leaders:

1. **Set clear, simple expectations**
   Clarity reduces stress and increases confidence.

2. **Celebrate effort and improvement**
   Reward progress, not perfection.

3. **Give frequent, honest feedback**
   Feedback is oxygen for growth.

4. **Remove unnecessary rules**
   Complexity kills motivation.

5. **Empower autonomy**
   Trust people to manage their work.
   Autonomy transforms engagement.

6. **Create rituals of recognition**
   Celebrate wins publicly and consistently.

7. **Address conflict quickly and respectfully**
   Unresolved tension poisons culture.

8. **Train leaders in emotional intelligence**
   IQ builds systems.
   EQ builds people.

9. **Encourage creativity and new ideas**
   Make innovation a norm, not an exception.

10. **Protect mental health**
    Leaders must model balance, clarity, and calmness.

HOW TO BUILD A HIGH-PERFORMANCE CULTURE AT HOME

Families also need:

- clarity
- communication
- encouragement
- expectations
- healthy boundaries
- emotional safety
- structure
- routines
- connection

Strong family culture produces confident, resilient children.

Here's how to build it:

1. Create a home of emotional safety

Children thrive where they feel respected and heard.

2. Establish daily or weekly family rituals

Dinner time
Game nights
Walks
Talk sessions
Decompression time

Rituals create connection.

3. Speak life, not discouragement

Your words shape their identity.

4. Apologize when needed

Parents gain influence through humility, not perfection.

5. Model discipline and excellence

Children copy what you consistently do.

6. Set clear expectations

Clarity creates confidence and reduces chaos.

7. Encourage strengths, not comparisons

Every child has a unique Genius Zone.

8. Protect mental health at home

Teach rest.
Teach boundaries.
Teach emotional regulation.

9. Teach problem-solving, not dependency

Guided independence builds leadership.

10. Build a culture of love

Love is the foundation of emotional intelligence, resilience, and confidence.

Love empowers excellence.
Fear suppresses it.

THE SECRET OF HIGH-PERFORMANCE CULTURE

High-performance culture is not about pressure—
it's about alignment.

Not about perfection—
but progress.

Not about control—
but empowerment.

Not about pushing harder—
but working smarter.

Not about forcing compliance—
but inspiring contribution.

When you build the right culture, everything else accelerates:

- performance
- retention
- creativity
- fulfillment
- teamwork
- innovation
- loyalty
- leadership development
- long-term success

Culture is the invisible force that shapes visible results.

Build it intentionally—at work and at home—
and you build people who rise higher than they ever imagined.

CHAPTER SIXTEEN

THE SECRET INGREDIENT: WHY HUMILITY ELEVATES LEADERS

Every generation celebrates strength, brilliance, charisma, and authority.

But the most underestimated and misunderstood leadership advantage—the one that transforms teams, builds loyalty, and sustains long-term success—is something almost no one talks about:

Humility.

Not weakness.
Not insecurity.
Not submission.
Not silence.

Humility is the quiet power that transforms leaders into legends.

It is the ability to stay grounded while you rise.
To stay teachable while you succeed.
To stay human while you lead.

In this chapter, we expose why humility is the most strategic leadership trait in the modern world—for CEOs, small business owners, government leaders, professionals, and parents.

HUMILITY IS NOT THINKING LESS OF YOURSELF—IT IS THINKING CLEARLY ABOUT YOURSELF

Humility is confidence without arrogance.
Strength without aggression.
Authority without ego.

Humility means:

- You know your strengths
- You admit your weaknesses
- You accept feedback
- You stay open to learning
- You don't pretend to know everything
- You stay approachable
- You remain realistic and aware
- You value people over position

Humble leaders don't shrink.
They elevate others—and in doing so, they rise even higher.

WHY HUMILITY IS A SUPERPOWER IN MODERN LEADERSHIP

Humility is no longer optional.
It is essential.

Here's why:

1. HUMILITY MAKES YOU ADAPTABLE

In a world changing faster than ever, rigid leaders break.
Adaptable leaders thrive.

Humility allows you to say:

- "I don't know."
- "Teach me."
- "Help me understand."
- "Let's rethink this."
- "Is there a better way?"

This mindset keeps you relevant.
Keeps you innovative.
Keeps you improving.

Ego locks leaders into the past.
Humility pulls them into the future.

2. HUMILITY BUILDS TRUST

People don't trust perfect leaders.
They trust authentic leaders.

A humble leader is:

- honest
- self-aware
- willing to listen
- willing to admit mistakes
- willing to course-correct

This builds credibility.
Credibility builds influence.
Influence builds loyalty.

Humble leaders don't demand loyalty—
they earn it.

3. HUMILITY STRENGTHENS TEAMS

When leaders operate from humility:

- people feel safe
- ideas flow freely
- creativity increases
- collaboration strengthens
- conflict decreases
- morale rises

Humility creates psychological safety—
the most important ingredient of high-performing teams.

When the leader's ego disappears,
the team's brilliance appears.

4. HUMILITY ACCELERATES LEARNING

Leaders who stop learning become leaders people stop following.

Humility says:

· "There's always more to learn."
· "Someone else may have a better idea."
· "Let's explore new solutions."

Humility is the fuel of growth.
It prevents stagnation.
It eliminates blind spots.
It expands intelligence.

The best leaders in the world remain students.

5. HUMILITY ATTRACTS TOP TALENT

Talented people don't want to work for controlling, arrogant leaders.
They want to work with leaders who:

· listen
· empower
· collaborate
· encourage
· value people

Humility communicates safety and respect—
two things top talent demands.

A humble CEO retains people.
An arrogant CEO repels them.

6. HUMILITY BALANCES AMBITION

Ambition without humility becomes reckless.
Humility without ambition becomes passive.

But ambition with humility becomes unstoppable.

It looks like:

- bold vision
- grounded execution
- high drive
- wise decision-making
- passionate leadership
- responsible growth

Humility doesn't weaken ambition—
it purifies it.

WHY EGO IS THE ENEMY OF LEADERSHIP

Ego produces:

- defensiveness
- stubbornness
- conflict
- insecurity
- poor decisions
- micromanagement
- resistance to feedback
- unhealthy culture

- blind spots
- bad hires
- bad partnerships

Ego kills organizations long before competition does.

Leaders don't fail because they aren't smart.
They fail because they can't get out of their own way.

THE HUMILITY GAP BETWEEN GENERATIONS

Here's something powerful:

The younger generation values humility in leaders far more than previous generations.

They want leaders who are:

- real
- honest
- empathetic
- collaborative
- human

They reject leaders who:

- pretend to know everything
- refuse to admit mistakes
- operate from intimidation
- lead by force
- command without connecting

This is not disrespect.
This is growth.

They are calling leaders to a higher standard—
one that elevates humanity over hierarchy.

HOW TO PRACTICE HUMILITY AS A LEADER

Here are simple, powerful shifts that build humble leadership:

1. **Listen before responding**
   Listening is the loudest form of humility.

2. **Ask for feedback often**
   Feedback is not a threat—it's a tool.

3. **Acknowledge when someone has a better idea**
   This builds collaboration and trust.

4. **Admit mistakes quickly and transparently**
   Mistakes don't destroy credibility—denial does.

5. **Give credit generously**
   Humble leaders shine the spotlight on others.

6. **Stay curious**
   Curiosity destroys arrogance.

7. **Don't pretend to be the smartest person in the room**
   Instead, build a room filled with smart people.

8. **Respect every role**

   From interns to executives.

   Respect elevates culture.

9. **Replace pride with purpose**

   Focus on the mission, not your image.

10. **Develop emotional intelligence**

    Self-awareness is the root of humility.

HUMILITY IS THE FOUNDATION OF ENDURING LEADERSHIP

History proves something powerful:

Arrogant leaders rise quickly and fall suddenly.
Humble leaders rise steadily and build legacies.

Because humility:

- deepens relationships
- strengthens teams
- improves decision-making
- expands self-awareness
- multiplies influence
- stabilizes leadership
- elevates culture
- inspires loyalty
- sustains long-term success

Humility is not weakness—
it is wisdom.

It is not timidity—
it is maturity.

It is not gentleness only—
it is greatness under control.

The leaders who embrace humility become leaders that nations, companies, families, and communities trust—and follow.

Because humility does not push people down.

Humility lifts people up.

And when leaders lift people up...
those people lift the leader even higher.

CHAPTER SEVENTEEN

THE COURAGE TO CHANGE: REINVENTING YOURSELF IN A RAPIDLY CHANGING WORLD

As I worked with leaders, CEOs, and entrepreneurs, I noticed something fascinating: the younger generation didn't respond to the old rules. They weren't interested in the grind, the hustle, or the decades of sacrifice that defined previous generations.

At first, I struggled to understand it.

Then one day, after a leadership session, a young woman approached me and said:

"We're not lazy.
We just refuse to lose ourselves the way your generation did."

Her honesty stunned me. It was bold, unfiltered... and true.

It made me reflect on my own life—how I worked myself to exhaustion believing it was the only way. And I realized something:

They were not rejecting work.
They were rejecting **meaningless** work.

They didn't want titles—they wanted purpose.
They didn't want more hours—they wanted impact.
They didn't want managers—they wanted mentors.

Suddenly, everything made sense.

This generation wasn't a problem.
They were a preview of the future.

Their values reshaped how I teach leadership.
They influenced the frameworks inside this book.
They forced me—and the world—to redefine success.

The world is evolving at a speed humanity has never experienced before.
Industries are shifting.
Technology is disrupting.
Jobs are disappearing.
New opportunities are emerging.
Expectations are transforming.

The only constant now is change—
and the greatest skill any leader, parent, professional, CEO, or business owner can possess is the courage to reinvent themselves.

Reinvention is not a luxury.
It is survival.
It is relevance.
It is the foundation of long-term success and meaningful impact.

This chapter is about how to transform—boldly, intelligently, strategically—no matter where you are in life.

THE BIGGEST BARRIER TO CHANGE ISN'T FEAR— IT'S FAMILIARITY

Most people don't stay stuck because the future scares them.
They stay stuck because the past comforts them.

Familiar routines.
Familiar habits.
Familiar environments.
Familiar beliefs.
Familiar identities.

People cling to the old not because it's working—
but because it's known.

But here's the truth:
Nothing grows in the comfort zone.

The comfort zone feels safe, but it keeps you small.
The growth zone feels uncomfortable, but it expands your potential.

Reinvention begins where familiarity ends.

WHY CHANGE FEELS SO HARD

Change threatens three things:

1. Your Identity

When you reinvent, you must let go of who you were to become who you can be.

That can feel uncomfortable—but it is necessary.

2. Your Routine

Change disrupts patterns that have shaped your behavior.

Your brain loves routines because they conserve energy, even if those routines are unproductive.

3. Your Security

Change introduces uncertainty.

But here's a powerful truth:

The illusion of security has destroyed more potential than the reality of risk ever has.

THE MOST SUCCESSFUL PEOPLE REINVENT CONSTANTLY

Look at world-class leaders:

They don't reinvent once.
They reinvent repeatedly.

Athletes reinvent their training.
CEOs reinvent their companies.
Entrepreneurs reinvent their strategies.
Innovators reinvent entire industries.
Professionals reinvent their skillsets.
Parents reinvent their leadership as children grow.

Reinvention is not a sign of instability—
it is a sign of intelligence.

The more willing you are to adapt,
the more powerful you become.

THE THREE LEVELS OF REINVENTION

Every transformation happens in three stages.

Master these, and you can reinvent anytime.

LEVEL 1: MINDSET REINVENTION

Reinvention begins internally.

You must change:

- how you think
- how you see yourself
- how you see the world
- what you believe is possible
- what you believe you deserve

The thoughts that carried you this far cannot carry you to your next level.

Your mindset must evolve before your life does.

LEVEL 2: HABIT REINVENTION

Your habits shape your identity, your performance, and your future.

Reinvention requires upgrading:

- what you consume
- how you work
- how you think
- how you plan
- how you prioritize
- how you recover
- how you communicate

Small shifts in daily habits create massive shifts in long-term outcomes.

LEVEL 3: IDENTITY REINVENTION

This is the highest level.

Identity reinvention means you no longer see yourself as:

- who you used to be
- what your past told you
- what others expect
- what past environments shaped

Identity reinvention is when you say:

"I am becoming someone new."
"I am capable of more."
"I am choosing the next version of myself."

The world responds to who you believe you are.

Reinvention requires choosing a new identity—and living into it.

THE COST OF REFUSING TO CHANGE

People don't get stuck because life is hard.
People get stuck because they refuse to evolve.

Refusing to change leads to:

- stagnation
- burnout
- irrelevance
- frustration
- resentment
- missed opportunities
- declining confidence
- declining performance

The world will move forward with or without you.

Reinvention is how you stay in the game—
and dominate it.

THE YOUNGER GENERATION EMBRACES CHANGE— AND THAT IS THEIR POWER

Many older leaders say:

"They jump too fast."
"They switch careers too often."
"They don't stay committed."
"They move too quickly."

But here's the truth:

The younger generation understands the new world better than anyone else.

They know:

- change is constant
- flexibility is strength
- reinvention is normal
- adaptability is advantage
- new skills are currency
- growth is endless

They are not unstable—
they are agile.

They are not uncertain—
they are evolving.

They are not confused—
they are experimental.

This is why they thrive in emerging industries, digital spaces, and innovation-driven environments.

Adaptability is their superpower.

THE FOUR REASONS MOST ADULTS STOP CHANGING

If reinvention is so powerful, why do people resist it?

Because of:

1. **Fear of failure**
    They fear embarrassment more than stagnation.

2. **Fear of judgment**
    They allow other people's opinions to shrink their potential.

3. **Fear of inadequacy**
    They fear they won't be good at something new.

4. **Fear of losing control**
    They prefer predictable misery over unpredictable possibility.

But here is the truth that sets people free:

Staying the same is the biggest risk of all.

HOW TO REINVENT YOURSELF—STEP BY STEP

Here is a proven process used by elite performers, CEOs, successful entrepreneurs, and evolving leaders worldwide:

STEP 1: Create a Clear Picture of Your Next Level

Not who you are—
but who you want to become.

Ask:

- What does the next version of me look like?
- How do they think?
- How do they lead?
- What do they do daily?
- What goals have they achieved?
- Your future needs a face.

STEP 2: Identify What Must Be Left Behind

Reinvention is not just about adding—
it is about eliminating.

Ask:

- What beliefs must I release?
- What habits no longer serve me?
- What environments hold me back?
- What identities must I outgrow?

You cannot become the next version of yourself while clinging to the older one.

STEP 3: Build New Systems

Systems shape identity.
Identity shapes results.

Create systems for:

- work
- learning
- recovery
- growth
- planning
- habits
- performance

Systems make reinvention sustainable.

STEP 4: Enter New Environments

If you want to become someone new, you must step into environments that stretch you.

Surround yourself with:

- people who think bigger
- leaders who challenge you
- environments that inspire you
- opportunities that elevate you
- mentors who expand you

Environment is more powerful than willpower.

STEP 5: Take Bold Action Before You Feel Ready

Reinvention happens in motion—
not in planning.

You do not become confident before you start.
You become confident because you start.

Courage is the bridge between who you are and who you are becoming.

THE FUTURE BELONGS TO THE REINVENTORS

In this new era, the people who rise will not be:

- the strongest
- the smartest
- the most educated
- the most connected

The people who rise will be:

- the most adaptable
- the most courageous
- the most flexible
- the most teachable
- the most willing to change

They evolve with the times.
They learn faster than they fear.
They shift before they are forced to shift.
They reinvent before they become irrelevant.

The future does not belong to those who hold on.

The future belongs to those who let go—and rise higher.

CHAPTER EIGHTEEN

THE LEGACY OF LEADERSHIP: BUILDING A LIFE THAT OUTLIVES YOU

Every person leaves a mark on the world.
Some marks fade quickly.
Others echo through generations.

But true leadership—real leadership—is not measured by the titles you held, the money you earned, the awards you received, or the businesses you built.

Real leadership is measured by legacy.

Legacy is the impact you leave behind.
Legacy is the influence that continues after you are gone.
Legacy is your contribution to the world's future.
Legacy is the story people will tell because of you.

Whether you are a CEO, a small business owner, a parent, a government leader, or a professional, your legacy is being written every day—intentionally or unintentionally.

This chapter explains how to build a legacy that inspires, empowers, and elevates people long after your season has ended.

LEGACY IS NOT WHAT YOU LEAVE FOR PEOPLE—IT IS WHAT YOU LEAVE IN PEOPLE

Money fades.
Positions fade.
Buildings fade.
Businesses shift.
Titles change.
Systems evolve.

But the impact you leave inside people—the wisdom, courage, confidence, inspiration, and empowerment—that is what lasts.

Legacy is not external.
Legacy is internal.

Legacy is not material.
Legacy is transformational.

THE THREE TYPES OF LEGACY EVERY LEADER CREATES

You are building a legacy in three domains, whether you realize it or not:

1. PERSONAL LEGACY

This is who you became as a person.

Your personal legacy is shaped by:

- Your values

- Your character
- Your habits
- Your integrity
- Your discipline
- Your courage
- Your mindset
- Your resilience

When people think of you, how do they feel?
Inspired?
Encouraged?
Respected?
Empowered?
Or stressed, intimidated, and unsafe?

Your personal legacy is the emotional imprint you leave.

2. RELATIONAL LEGACY

This is how you treated people.

Your relational legacy is shaped by:

- Your kindness
- Your empathy
- Your communication
- your ability to listen
- how you resolve conflict
- how you encourage others
- how you bring out the best in people

People remember how you made them feel long after they forget what you said.

The strongest legacies are built through relationships.

3. IMPACT LEGACY

This is what you contributed to the world.

Your impact legacy includes:

- businesses you built
- communities you strengthened
- people you mentored
- problems you solved
- innovations you created
- opportunities you opened
- systems you improved
- lives you changed

Impact is not measured in size—
impact is measured in significance.

LEGACY IS NOT AGE-DEPENDENT—IT IS DECISION-DEPENDENT

You do not build legacy at the end of life.
You build it in the middle—in the everyday moments that seem small but shape everything.

Legacy is built when you:

- choose growth over comfort
- choose people over ego
- choose excellence over mediocrity
- choose courage over fear
- choose kindness over indifference
- choose purpose over pressure
- Legacy is created through consistent decisions.
- Every choice is a brushstroke on the canvas of your future.

LEADERS WHO FAIL LEAVE BEHIND ACCIDENTAL LEGACIES

When leaders refuse to grow, lead with ego, or ignore the impact they are having, they leave behind legacies of:

- fear
- stress
- broken trust
- bitterness
- confusion
- resentment
- dysfunction

Accidental legacies are always negative.
Intentional legacies are always positive.

You cannot control everything,
but you can control how you lead.

THE FOUR CHARACTERISTICS OF LEGACY LEADERS

Legacy leaders are remembered because of four defining traits:

1. VISION

They see beyond the moment.
They think long-term.
They build for the future, not for applause.

2. COURAGE

They make bold decisions.
They stand for something meaningful.
They act even when afraid.

3. GENEROSITY

They give their wisdom, time, attention, and opportunity freely.
They multiply others, not just themselves.

4. INTEGRITY

They are the same person privately and publicly.
Their words and actions match.

THE YOUNGER GENERATION CARES ABOUT LEGACY MORE THAN SUCCESS

Today's young people are not asking:

"How do I become successful?"

They are asking:

"How do I make an impact?"
"How do I live authentically?"
"How do I change the world?"
"How do I leave something meaningful behind?"

They value:

- purpose over profit
- contribution over competition
- authenticity over image
- alignment over tradition

This mindset requires parents, leaders, and organizations to think differently.

Legacy is not optional in the new world—
it is essential.

THE FOUR BUILDING BLOCKS OF A LEGENDARY LEGACY

Here is the formula:

1. **CHARACTER**
   Your values become your foundation.

2. **CONTRIBUTION**
   Your strengths become your gift to the world.

3. **CONNECTION**
   Your relationships become your influence.

4. CONTINUITY

Your actions inspire others to carry your mission forward.

THE LEGACY YOU BUILD AT HOME IS THE MOST IMPORTANT OF ALL

Whether you are a parent or not, you are influencing the next generation.

Legacy at home is built through:

- patience
- presence
- listening
- guidance
- example
- kindness
- consistency
- mentorship
- emotional safety
- support

Homes shape identities.
Identities shape futures.
Futures shape nations.

Your legacy begins at home.

THE LEGACY YOU BUILD IN BUSINESS IS YOUR PROFESSIONAL FOOTPRINT

Your business legacy is not your profits.
It is your principles.

It is not the growth charts.
It is the people you elevated.

It is not your empire.
It is your impact.

People leave companies—
but they never forget leaders who changed their lives.

If you build people, you build legacy.
If you build legacy, you build immortality.

THE SECRET TO A LASTING LEGACY: LIVE IT EVERY DAY

You do not need to wait until the end of your life to build legacy.

You build legacy when you:

- say an encouraging word
- help someone believe in themselves
- solve a problem
- create an opportunity
- show kindness when it is difficult
- choose integrity when no one is watching

- empower the next generation
- lead with humility and courage

Legacy is created in small moments that become big memories.

LEGACY IS THE FINAL MEASURE OF TRUE LEADERSHIP

Not your salary.
Not your status.
Not your awards.
Not your popularity.
Not your possessions.

Your legacy is the story others will tell because of your life.

Will they say:

"You made them feel seen."
"You changed their direction."
"You unlocked their potential."
"You created opportunity."
"You led with love and courage."
"You made the world better."

The world changes not because of what leaders take—
but because of what leaders give.

Legacy is generosity expressed through leadership.

It is the final gift you leave behind.

CONCLUSION

CHAPTER NINETEEN

SUCCESS REIMAGINED: A NEW DEFINITION FOR A NEW WORLD

For decades, the world has used a narrow, outdated, and incomplete definition of success.

A definition shaped by:

- external validation
- cultural pressure
- material accumulation
- status symbols
- comparison
- busyness
- burnout
- blind ambition
- fear of falling behind

And because of this limited definition, millions of people have worked hard their entire lives...

yet remain unfulfilled, exhausted, and uncertain about what it all really meant.

But as we stand at the edge of a new era—
a digital era, a creative era, a mental era—
it's time to redefine what success truly is.

We need a definition that empowers, not exhausts.
One that uplifts, not overwhelms.
One that brings clarity, not confusion.
One that aligns with purpose, not pressure.

This chapter delivers that redefinition.

Welcome to *Success Reimagined*.

THE PROBLEM WITH THE OLD DEFINITION OF SUCCESS

The old definition of success was based on:

- accumulation
- achievement
- appearance
- approval
- comparison
- conformity

It measured people by:

- job titles
- income brackets
- possessions

- awards
- degrees
- popularity
- social acceptance
- The problem?

These measures say nothing about:

- fulfillment
- joy
- purpose
- alignment
- growth
- mental health
- impact
- relationships
- contribution
- authenticity

The old definition creates winners who feel like losers, and achievers who feel empty.

It creates exhausted professionals, stressed parents, disconnected families, burned-out executives, and generations who question the meaning of their effort.

Success, as we knew it, was incomplete.

THE NEW DEFINITION: SUCCESS IS A LIFE THAT WORKS

Success is not about how much you earn.
It is about how much you evolve.

Success is not about what you have.
It is about who you are becoming.

Success is not about status.
It is about stability—emotional, mental, relational, financial, spiritual, and personal.

Success is not about climbing a ladder.
It is about building a life that aligns with your deepest values.

Success is not external admiration.
Success is internal peace.

Success is not measured by applause.
Success is measured by impact.

Success is not the destination.
Success is the design of a life that works—a life that is balanced, aligned, meaningful, and lived with intention.

That is Success Reimagined.

THE FIVE PILLARS OF SUCCESS REIMAGINED

To build this new definition, we shift from shallow metrics to deep principles.

Here are the five pillars:

1. ALIGNMENT

Success begins when your life matches your identity.

Alignment means:

- You work in your strengths
- You honor your values
- You pursue what matters
- You stop living for approval
- You make choices that reflect who you are becoming

Alignment is the opposite of conflict.
It is the foundation of peace.

2. PURPOSE

A successful life is a purposeful life.

Purpose gives direction.
Purpose gives meaning.
Purpose gives courage.
Purpose gives you a reason to rise every morning.

Purpose transforms work from a burden into a contribution.

Without purpose, success feels empty.
With purpose, even challenges become meaningful.

3. GROWTH

Success is not about reaching a peak.
It is about continuous evolution.

A successful person is someone who is:

- learning
- improving
- stretching
- expanding
- upgrading
- adapting
- growing

Growth turns potential into power.
Growth is how you become the best version of yourself.

4. WELL-BEING

True success includes:

- mental health
- emotional balance
- physical wellness
- healthy relationships
- rest
- clarity
- joy

Success that destroys your well-being is not success—
it is self-sabotage wrapped in achievement.

Success Reimagined values wholeness over weariness.

5. IMPACT

Success is not what you gain—
it is what you give.

Impact is:

- what you contribute
- who you help
- the lives you change
- the opportunities you create
- the people you elevate
- the legacy you leave

Impact turns success into significance.

When your life becomes bigger than your personal ambition, you step into leadership.

WHY THE YOUNGER GENERATION ALREADY LIVES THIS NEW DEFINITION

Older generations were trained to pursue:

- security
- stability
- titles
- pensions
- external success

Younger generations pursue:

- meaning
- flexibility
- identity
- creativity
- contribution

They don't want to "look successful."
They want to feel successful.

They aren't chasing status.
They're chasing fulfillment.

They aren't prioritizing employers.
They're prioritizing alignment.

They aren't burning out for approval.
They're prioritizing mental health.

They didn't abandon success—
they redefined it.

And with this redefinition, they are building lives that actually work.

THE COST OF CHASING THE OLD SUCCESS

Those who cling to the old definition often experience:

- exhaustion
- emptiness
- resentment
- stress

- poor health
- loneliness
- unfulfillment
- broken relationships
- burnout

Success that costs you everything is not success—
it is loss disguised as accomplishment.

There is a better way.

THE FREEDOM OF SUCCESS REIMAGINED

When success is redefined as:

- alignment
- purpose
- growth
- well-being
- impact
- everything changes.

You begin to:

- work smarter
- live healthier
- love deeper
- think clearer
- lead stronger
- contribute greater
- feel fulfilled

- experience peace
- walk in authenticity
- build legacy

Success becomes sustainable.
Success becomes joyful.
Success becomes human.

HOW TO IMPLEMENT SUCCESS REIMAGINED IN YOUR LIFE

Here are practical steps for any leader, parent, professional, or entrepreneur:

1. Redefine your metrics.

Measure what truly matters, not what society pressures.

2. Audit your alignment.

Ask:
"Does my life match my values?"

3. Pursue purpose over pressure.

Choose a path that energizes you, not drains you.

4. Build routines that protect well-being.

Rest, recovery, clarity, and mindset shape high performance.

5. Expand your growth zone.

Learn something every day.

6. Contribute intentionally.

Impact is the highest form of achievement.

7. Eliminate unnecessary expectations.

Not every weight is worth carrying.

8. Celebrate progress, not perfection.

Success is a journey of becoming, not a race to the finish.

9. Prioritize relationships.

Success without strong relationships is failure in disguise.

10. Live boldly yet authentically.

Your life is your message.
Live a message worth remembering.

SUCCESS REIMAGINED IS A GIFT TO YOURSELF— AND TO THE WORLD

Because when you live in alignment, purpose, growth, well-being, and impact:

- You lead better
- You love better
- You think clearer
- You inspire others
- You elevate your family
- You uplift your team

- You transform your community
- You strengthen your organization
- You build legacy

Success Reimagined is not just a personal philosophy. It is a global solution to a tired, stressed, outdated understanding of success.

It gives people permission to live fully, work wisely, lead powerfully, and rest intentionally.

This is the success model that will dominate the future.

And it begins with you.

CHAPTER TWENTY

EPILOGUE

THE CALL TO RISE: YOUR INVITATION TO A REIMAGINED LIFE

Every book ends,
but a new life begins.

You've explored the ideas.
You've examined the principles.
You've seen the future of work, leadership, purpose, and success
through a new lens—
a lens that honors humanity, creativity, alignment, well-being,
impact, and smart work.

Now, this final chapter is not information.
It is an invitation.

An invitation to rise into the next version of yourself.
To redefine your potential.
To transform your path.
To unlock your Genius Zone.
To lead with intention.

To live with clarity.
To contribute with purpose.
To build a legacy that outlives you.

This is your moment.

THE WORLD IS CHANGING—AND SO MUST YOU

We are entering a new era.
An era where:

- Smart work outperforms hard work
- Creativity outshines conformity
- Mental wellness outranks mental toughness
- Identity outweighs tradition
- Purpose matters more than pressure
- Freedom fuels excellence
- Alignment replaces exhaustion
- Humanity becomes the heart of leadership

The world does not need more people who simply survive.

It needs people who rise.

People who bring innovation, clarity, compassion, courage, and contribution into the spaces they occupy.

People who think differently.
People who care deeply.
People who lead boldly.
People like you.

THE MOST IMPORTANT QUESTION YOU MUST ASK NOW

After reading this book, ask yourself:

"What will I do with what I now know?"

Knowledge without application is noise.
Knowledge with action is transformation.

You have insights that can shift your:

- career
- business
- leadership
- relationships
- purpose
- habits
- mindset
- future

But these insights only become power when they become practice.

This is your call to act.

THREE DECISIONS THAT WILL CHANGE YOUR LIFE FOREVER

If you apply nothing else from this book, apply this:

1. DECIDE TO LIVE IN ALIGNMENT

Stop living by other people's expectations.
Stop shrinking yourself to fit old systems.
Stop forcing yourself into roles that drain you.

Live a life that reflects your identity, your strengths, your purpose, and your Genius Zone.

Alignment is where excellence begins.

2. DECIDE TO EVOLVE CONSISTENTLY

The world changes.
You must change with it.

Reinvent.
Upgrade.
Adapt.
Learn.
Grow.
Stretch.
Rise.

Your evolution is your responsibility.

3. DECIDE TO LEAVE A LEGACY, NOT JUST A LIFE

Legacy is built through contribution.

Speak life into others.
Create opportunities.
Solve problems.
Build systems.
Lift people higher.
Lead with humility.
Love with courage.

Live in a way that others are better because you existed.

YOUR FUTURE IS CALLING

A reimagined life is not something you find.
It is something you build.

You build it:

- thought by thought
- habit by habit
- decision by decision
- day by day
- moment by moment

Greatness is not a moment.
Greatness is a direction.

And now you have a new direction.

A higher direction.
A smarter direction.
A healthier direction.
A more purposeful direction.

THE WORLD NEEDS WHAT YOU CARRY

Your experiences.
Your strengths.
Your creativity.
Your voice.
Your ideas.
Your leadership.
Your compassion.
Your innovation.
Your identity.
Your contribution.

There is a unique brilliance inside you—
something only you can give the world.

No one else can deliver it.
No one else can steward it.
No one else can express it.

You are irreplaceable.

And the world is waiting for you to rise.

THIS IS YOUR MOMENT TO CHOOSE

You can return to the old way:
working harder, burning out, chasing success, and living misaligned.

Or you can embrace the new way:
working smarter, living fuller, leading stronger, and walking in alignment with your purpose, strengths, and identity.

The choice is yours.

But one choice leads to exhaustion.
The other leads to elevation.

One leads to pressure.
The other leads to peace.

One leads to survival.
The other leads to significance.

One leads to a life lived.
The other leads to a legacy earned.

Choose the life that reimagines your future.
Choose the path that honors who you are becoming.
Choose the world that needs your contribution.

Choose to rise.

THE CALL TO RISE

You were not born to be average.
You were not born to blend in.
You were not born to simply exist.

You were born to elevate.
To evolve.
To inspire.
To innovate.
To lead.
To create.
To contribute.
To impact.
To transform.

You were born to rise.

This is your invitation.
This is your moment.

Welcome to your reimagined life.

Success Reimagined begins with you.

Your friend, Melvin Pillay

P.S. I would love to hear all about your journey! Don't hesitate to drop me a line and share your thoughts with me at success@melvin-pillay.com. I look forward to connecting with you.

ABOUT THE AUTHOR

Melvin Pillay is an internationally recognized speaker, author, leadership strategist, and transformational coach whose work has impacted thousands across the United States and around the world. Born and raised in the racial and economic oppression of apartheid South Africa, Melvin's early life was marked by poverty, limitation, and systemic injustice. Yet from that adversity, he developed the resilience, hunger, and inner fire that would become the foundation of his extraordinary journey.

Determined to break generational barriers, Melvin rose from humble beginnings to become a highly sought-after executive coach and organizational strategist. Over the past 25 years, he has trained CEOs, professionals, entrepreneurs, government leaders, and high-performance teams—equipping them to think differently, work wisely, and lead with purpose.

As the founder of **The UNWORK Revolution**, **The Smart Work Matrix**, and the **Kingdom Millionaires Academy**, Melvin has built a reputation for helping people unlock their potential, maximize their identity, and step boldly into their destiny. His unique ability to combine practical leadership systems with deep personal insight has made him a trusted voice in boardrooms, universities, faith communities, and global platforms.

Melvin's message is born not from theory, but from lived experience.
From escaping the limitations of apartheid...
to overcoming poverty...
to achieving corporate success...
to burning out as a workaholic...
to discovering a new, life-giving definition of success.

It is this journey of transformation that shaped *Success Reimagined*, his groundbreaking framework for living and leading in a rapidly changing world.

More than a speaker or strategist, Melvin is a voice of clarity in an age of confusion—a guide for those seeking purpose, alignment, and high-impact living. His work empowers readers and audiences to rise above the old rules of success and embrace a new model built on identity, purpose, and sustainable excellence.

Melvin lives in Washington, DC, where he continues to write, teach, build leaders, and inspire individuals to elevate their lives and transform their world.

MELVIN'S PROGRAMS

The *Smart Work* Matrix with Melvin

Are you ready to work smart with Melvin, unlearn the junk, un-grind from the rat race, understand yourself, and be free?

Melvin is available for keynote talks and offers several Easy and Light consulting, coaching, and mastermind programs worldwide.

The Whiteboard Session with Melvin Pillay

The Whiteboard Session is an immersive and transformative experience that integrates spiritual, mental, emotional, and practical dimensions. It is all aimed at optimizing personal development and preparing individuals for their destined path. This session is meticulously structured to facilitate the transition from potential to realization, offering profound insights into establishing a legacy that can endure for future generations.

A hallmark of the Whiteboard Session is its personalized approach.

Each session is tailored for each participant, ensuring no two experiences are identical. The process is guided by divine revelation rather than solely depending on human wisdom or knowledge, fostering a spiritually enriching environment conducive to authentic growth and self-discovery. Over the past two decades, Melvin Pillay has engaged with diverse clients, including prominent business figures, innovative entrepreneurs, and influential government leaders. Through a unique coaching format, he has assisted individuals in unlocking their latent potential, guiding them toward realizing their fullest capabilities.

During the Whiteboard Session, participants can anticipate an in-depth engagement with the following key components:

1. *Exploration of Your Timeline:* Participants will collaboratively examine their life timeline, reflecting on past experiences, assessing their current circumstances, and envisioning their future aspirations. This exploration aims to uncover significant promises and purposes integral to the individual's life journey.
2. *Identification and Activation of Gifts:* Individuals will have the opportunity to identify their unique gifts and talents. More importantly, there will be a focus on activating these strengths to foster enhanced confidence and clarity in their abilities.
3. *Assessment of Journey Conditions:* It is essential to understand the conditions that influence one's personal path. An evaluation of the physical, emotional, and spiritual environments in which individuals operate will be conducted to recognize factors that may facilitate or hinder progress.
4. *Uncovering Obstacles:* Participants will collaboratively identify barriers or obstacles currently impeding their progress. By illuminating these challenges, effective strategies can be developed to overcome them, ensuring a smoother path forward.

5. *Strategic Blueprint Development:* While examining visions and aspirations, a comprehensive strategic blueprint will be collaboratively created. This actionable plan will serve as a guide for participants to install lasting values and principles that will resonate for years to come.

6. *Foundation for Family Legacy:* In addition to personal fulfillment, emphasis will also be placed on establishing a robust foundational legacy for families and future generations. This component aims to empower participants to instill lasting values and principles that will resonate for years to come.

The Whiteboard Session transcends a standard coaching experience; it constitutes a significant step toward realizing one's God-given potential and establishing a legacy that positively influences others. Participants are encouraged to come prepared to explore, discover, and activate the possibilities within themselves.

Life After Success

"Life After Success" is a comprehensive program meticulously designed to optimize key dimensions for high achievers, public figures, CEOs, and business owners. This initiative aims to help individuals navigate the often-overlooked transition from success to true significance in their lives.

Uncover Your True Identity—Who am I?

Unlock Your Destiny—Where am I coming from?

Understand Your Authority—What am I anointed for?

Participants will engage with rich, thought-provoking content that explores the deeper meanings of success and addresses critical questions related to legacy and purpose. The program offers structured insights and actionable strategies for creating a lasting impact that transcends personal accolades and financial achievement. Through an integrated approach that includes workshops, reflective activities, and collaborative discussions, attendees will discover how to leverage their accomplishments to cultivate a greater sense of community, influence, and fulfillment.

By focusing on these essential areas, "Life After Success" equips participants with the tools and mindset necessary to craft a legacy that resonates and endures, ultimately leading to a more enriched and purposeful existence.

For more information, please reach us at
support@melvinpillay.com.

www.melvinpillay.com

www.ingramcontent.com/pod-product-compliance
Lightning Source LLC
Chambersburg PA
CBHW071415180526
45170CB00001B/108